WAITING FOR YOU

THINGS WE SHOULD ALL THINK ABOUT!

by George S. Newton

A Study in Character, Morality, and Ethics

Utilizing Lessons from the Bible

Facts from World and U.S. History, plus

Memorial Scenes from American Literature

As its Textbook

Library of Congress Control Number:		2010906027
ISBN:	Hardcover	978-1-4500-9329-3
	Softcover	978-1-4500-9328-6

To order additional copies of this book, contact:
Xlibris Corporation
1-888-795-4274
www.Xlibris.com
Orders@Xlibris.com
47881

This work is dedicated to all those who care; especially my wife Barbara, whose faith and support made me want to become her Roman Catholic husband.

A special thanks to the staff and student body of Putnam City Original High School in Oklahoma City, especially those in the class of 2010; some of whom I served as their guest teacher when they were in the 6th grade. Their interest and encouragement gave me special incentives to work for them. I wish them all the best in the years to come and pray they will always just do "what's right".

Contents

To Eldora,

May God continue to
Bless you forever. Enjoy

Best Wishes,

Wayne Newton

Love you Mom,
God Bless You
Love Dahlia
(contrast)

PREFACE

I think many of us from time to time have thought about death, have felt lonely, have had the feeling that nobody cares, or have just felt discouraged. These are horrible feelings for sure and seem to always haunt us when we are experiencing hard times. The Renaissance, for example, was a time that was filled with a vivid awareness of human mortality due to the spread of the plague. It would have been very common to reflect on one's life during these terrible times.

The English poet, John Donne, however, who lived during these times, would not become discouraged about anything because of his great amount of religious faith. From his work, "Meditation XVII," Donne wrote two observations about death versus participation, which are often quoted. In his "Holy Sonnet 10" he says, "Death, be not proud, though some have called thee Mighty and dreadful, for thou art not so." Death itself was not so much a terrible event to be feared, he concluded, but more of an honor, a passing from a worst life to a better one, something which was to be joyously anticipated. "One short sleep past, we wake eternally, and Death shall be no more; Death, thou shalt die." From "Meditation XVII," he writes "And Perchance he for whom this bell tolls, may be so ill, as that he knows not it tolls for him; and perchance I may think myself so much better never send to know for whom the bell tolls, it tolls for thee."

In the same work, he addresses the theme of isolation. John Donne felt that no one could exist on his own, cut off from the rest of society. He wrote, "No man is an island, entire of itself; every man is a piece of the continent, a part of the main; if a clod be washed away by the sea, Europe is the less . . . any man's death diminishes me, because I am involved in mankind."

The good news for believers in Christ is "you will live forever and never walk alone!" Jesus died for our sins so we could have everlasting life; he is with us always. By his grace, you can find peace, love, and wisdom and share these virtues with others. It is therefore my prayer that this book will somehow help you to discover the gift of freedom and love, which God has bestowed on all believers, and how to use them. It was Micah who said, "You have been told, O man, what is good, and what the Lord requires of you. Peace be with you as you journey towards the end; where, He'll be, 'Waiting For You.'"

Yours in Christ,
George S. Newton

INTRODUCTION

Waiting for You: Things We Should All Think About focuses on the importance of building a strong character based on universally accepted religious principles, morals, and ethics. By utilizing stories and wisdom from the Christian Bible, themes and scenes from some of the best American novels, as well as historical facts from World and U.S. History—including many opinions and philosophies that have their roots in a Christian ethic—it is hoped that readers will be inspired to keep God first in their life, will become a social advocate for the common good, and will want to be the type of friend everyone desires. It seems to me, if we as a society rediscover what Christian morality and ethics mean we will be inspired to find that which has been lost and must be found again. There doesn't seem to be anything these days to inspire us to want to become a more productive citizen, to set goals that will show us the way to being a more beneficial player in today's society or a champion of the common good, unless there is something in it for us.

Lots of people today are desperately being challenged to find ways to rebuild the losses they have incurred from their retirement plans, survive the loss of income from being laid off, or feverishly trying to procure alternative and extra jobs to win back their sense of importance and dignity caused by the effects of company merges, downsizing, or bankruptcies. Those whose home values continue to go down have less equity with which to seek refinancing to a lower interest rate. Lenders are reluctant to refinance mortgages to lower rates because of the uncertainty of market conditions. Repaying loans, credit card debt, and home mortgage payments are creating unbelievable financial stress on our society. It is almost incomprehensible what is happening to our economy. We are indeed experiencing hard times, and it is time to make some hard changes.

Maybe this is the time to consider making a few changes in your life as well, changes that will help you realize that living within one's means is a good thing. Maybe we should be more faithful to our Christian beliefs and practice becoming more of a champion for the common good, the friend everyone desires, a social advocate for those who need help, or the one who is admired and called reliable because of their integrity.

It's time we recognize that by promoting the need to develop Christian principles as part of God's "will" and by focusing on these principles, we will learn that God's real gift to us is "freedom"! Freedom to make good choices instead of "knowledge" for the procurement of power. By making good choices and practicing Christian morality and ethics, we will experience how it is possible to make life exciting again.

Special discussions in this book focus on such questions as what constitutes a person's character. What does it mean to be called a person of integrity? What should the role of a productive citizen be? How does a person's ethical behavior build integrity or are they the same thing? Why should we care about others? What are the benefits of establishing a moral and ethical attitude? Why put God back in our life? How can we make better decisions? Why is it important to be able to have good communication skills? All of these discussions challenge readers to master some very ambitious goals, especially if they are interested in making changes in their life.

All too often, when we face new challenges, a sense of "Am I ready for this?" creeps up and projects an aura of anxiousness in our personality, especially when it involves an unknown outcome. Young adults, for example, have questions like, what kind of job can I find? Or, what will my first job be like after graduation? Is that all it pays? Will I be able to handle college work, or should I join the military first, then go to college? Should I go to a trade school or vocational-technical school to learn a trade so I can start to earn a living? Young married couples wonder if they should wait until they get their finances in order before having a family. Should I take that job in another state and leave behind my friends and family? Then there are those who seem to have it all together. They know what they want to do, where they are going, and have the money or scholarships to pay the tuition required or the skills and credentials to land the big position. A job to them becomes spending money.

Life can certainly be frustrating, not just for the young teenager or young adult but for all of us. Why do you suppose we always admire those who have the ability to inspire and motivate others, those whose thinking and actions always seem to be positive, or those who can motivate and influence others to use their talents for the good of the cause? It is because we want to be like them. The act of helping others can be a wonderful personal accomplishment. We can see how happy they are in their eyes, the way they smile at us, and above all, by the way they treat others. To know that you have been a positive influence on someone who wanted to be someone they thought that they could not be becomes a point of conversation for years to come while trying to motivate the next one. Don't we always feel better on our way home from a pleasant experience with someone who was kind, polite, caring, and helpful while providing us with their service? Aren't we happy to see others succeed when we knew in our hearts that they had the potential to become a more productive person?

When people make positive changes in their attitude and change the methods by which they deal with everyday tasks, their behavior becomes more pleasant and addictive. They begin to find their role as being more important and becoming more productive. When people respond to their kindness, professionalism, and dedication to their profession, they soon see the task of providing services to others as routine. To them, every day is a challenge to be better than yesterday and more pleasant to their customers. For them, helping others reach their goal gives them pride and helps them to recognize they are associated with class. Persons with a Christian morality and a strong work ethic usually attract like associates, which customers relate to. People, regardless of their ability, who are too concerned about the hand they have been dealt with rather than focusing on their positive energies and talents seem to be called losers. This book is dedicated to those who want to feel that their life is important and especially for those who want to know how to make a difference in one's life.

In the Old Testament, God used the prophet as his representative to speak to the people. We are taught that the prophet is someone who speaks out of a strong conviction and with a sense of vocation and sense of urgency. But like most prophets, faced with enormous opposition and a lonely voice, the prophet's job of communicating God's love for his people and to warn them of his concern for their soul was not well received. The prophet's challenge to confront the task of teaching the principles God wanted his people to live by was always being denounced by the unmoral and spiritually broken people of their day. The prophet, because of his personal relationship with God, constantly renounced the sinfulness in his community and encouraged his people to repent and change their lives—from a selfish concern for their own being to those who are poor, ill, or alone. His message was often too unpopular and painful for the people to give much serious consideration, but the prophet was obliged to warn the community of the consequences. Whether the concerns of the day were social, political, or religious in nature, the prophet's challenge was to communicate God's message. As Abraham J. Heschel writes in his wonderful book, *The Prophets*, "The two staggering facts in the life of a prophet are: God's turning to him, and man's turning away from him. This is often his lot: to be chosen by God and to be rejected by the people. The Word of God, so clear to him, is unintelligible to them." **(1)**

I believe, as did the prophet, that we should not forget the will of God in our life. Our society needs to make a concerted effort to understand the importance of God's virtues, to help others when they know and see that someone needs their advice, friendship, influence, or kindness. We need to respect human dignity and emphasize living by Christian principles of morality, integrity, and ethics with the same sense of urgency. I think it is important for all of us to want to be like the prophet who had an urgent message. To be a special friend, an advisor, a mentor, an example of a person with a strong character, a person who lives by practicing Christian morals and ethical principles should be our goal. It feels good to be the one who can discuss and demonstrate by example what it takes to suggest alternative actions with confidence. When one is able to genuinely reflect a desire to help others solve problems, attitudes change from a hostile disbelief to cooperative action. Sometimes we just need to know that someone cares about our problems and will not try to compound our discouragement by making us listen to their problems.

Sometimes, all it takes to become a positive influence on another's life is the ability to give constructive but helpful advice in a caring manner while being mindful and respectful of the other person's feelings. To give a helping hand without conditions releases the pressure from the one in need. "Kindness, justice, and righteousness are heaven's part in life," says Heschel. Others will want to be like you when you show them how you can handle problems with ease. Because of your spiritual attitude, you will be able to demonstrate a confidence that God is there for you now and always. The life you live should demonstrate your endorsement of God's principles thus making you a person to be trusted, relied upon, worthy of friendship, and respected. When those you are trying to help realize your qualities, you will personally experience a change in their attitude from suspicion to respect. You will smile with confidence when others start asking for your suggestions about solving a problem. It is the prophet Jeremiah who reminds us of what the Lord said when others cherish wisdom, wealth, and power over charity, morality, and respect:

> Let not the wise man glory in his wisdom, nor the strong man glory in his strength, nor the rich man glory in his riches; But rather, let him who glories, glory in this, that in his prudence he knows me,
> Knows that I, the Lord, brings about kindness, justice, and uprightness on the earth: for with such am I pleased says the Lord. (Jer. 9:22-23, NAB)

Heschel says, "Knowledge of God is knowledge of what He does: kindness, justice, righteousness." He continues, "The phenomenon of prophecy is predicated upon the assumption that man is both in need of, and entitled to, divine guidance. For God to reveal His word through the prophet to His people is an act of justice or an act of seeking to do justice. The purpose of prophecy is to maintain the covenant, to establish the right relationship between God and man" (*The Prophet*, p. 202).

Ask yourself, what are your personal strengths? How effectively do you think you project the image of being a person of integrity? How do you perceive your role as a productive citizen? Have you examined the value of supporting and practicing a religion that advocates peace, love, and respect for human dignity? What does advocating peace, love, and respect for human dignity mean to our community and to us?

It is my hope that you will support the attitude that says we want to accomplish this "for the common good" because serving the "common good" is the most important social purpose we have, in my opinion, that will help to stimulate the concepts of peace, cooperation, and justice for all within any community. A person who projects an image of being a person of integrity, whose behavior reflects the best interest of the common good, and one who supports and lives by the principles of a religious theology is certainly a champion of this social cause because we know solutions are more apt to become a reality when they have been morally and ethically derived and reflect the best interest of the common good.

It is also a goal of this book to suggest that readers should want to develop their academic desire to think analytically and develop an effective method of meaningful communications. Being able to project a logical, intellectually confident, and positive tone in one's conversation establishes one's sincerity and serves to support a sincere attitude in their effort to promote those solutions, which are in the interest of the most people. Presentations, orally or written, which are easily understood, written or spoken without evidence of prejudice and purposefully designed to be flexible enough to accommodate future adjustments should be communicated well. How does one begin such a project? Maybe we should start by taking a serious look at the direction our society is going today and discern such questions as

Do you think people's moral attitude and behavior today is

> . . . a reflection of poor academic and social accomplishments,
> . . . a lack of opportunity or desire to want to make changes, or
> . . . simply a result of a promiscuous philosophy that says, as long as it doesn't effect me, it's okay.

Do you think the task of making a community a better place to live in is a task most people feel is important enough to want to accomplish? And if so, do they have the ambition, ability, and proper incentive to want to do it?

Other important concepts regarding the makeup of a person's life, which I think need to be revisited, includes

- the role, in our everyday life, that moral and ethical principles play;
- what it means to be a person of integrity;
- the importance of belonging to a religion that advocates peace, love, and respect for human dignity; and
- why it is important to develop an attitude that says, "We should promote the common good as one of our most important social goals."

The answers to these concepts and principles, I believe, make you aware of what needs to change in our thinking and how we need to rid ourselves of the "if it doesn't affect me" attitude so often displayed as the nucleus for making today's life choices. When one gives serious thought to the questions like, what are the most important tools required for making effective decisions, formulating principles to live by, and the key factors in successfully dealing with others especially in today's multicultural society, a strong suggestion should be made that the reader work to expand their usage and knowledge of what makes a person of character a better family member, friend, business associate, and citizen. When developed to their fullest, Christian morality, integrity, ethics, and character will help people to recognize the future as an opportunity to create what is in the best interest of the common good and a way to make life exciting again for them.

In my opinion, there exists today a strong need to put God back in our lives. Men and women of character always thank God for their gifts, which have led them to accomplish great things. In the chapter "Making a Case for Religious Education," we explore the need to support a religion of one's choice. You will also find that there is a strong emphasis on the importance of maintaining the need for spiritual as well as academic education. In the last chapter, I take the opportunity to nominate "love" as being the best choice a person can make as their cornerstone for achieving happiness and also make the suggestion that "freedom" is the reason why "justice for all" should become the major ingredient in making this a more congenial global community. Finally, it is my sincere hope that you will give some thought to the "THINGS TO THINK ABOUT" comments highlighted at the end of each chapter.

THINK ABOUT IT:

FOR OUR FREEDOM AND BLESSINGS, WE SHOULD THANK GOD.

"Freedom is given to man by the Creator as a gift and at the same time as a task. Through freedom, man is called to accept and to implement the truth regarding the good." **(2)**

FOR THE OPPORTUNITY TO LIVE IN A FREE COUNTRY SO BLESSED BY GOD'S LOVE, WE SHOULD THANK A SOLDIER!

"Gathering in the church at 10:30 on the morning of Saturday March 4, 1944, the President of the United States, his Cabinet, and the senior officials of a nation at war bowed there heads as these words were said:

> *'Most loving Father, who by thy Son Jesus Christ hast taught us to love our enemies and to pray for them, we beseech thee, give to those who are now our enemies the light of thy Holy Spirit. Grant that they and we, being enlightened in conscience and cleansed from every sin, may now and do thy will, and so be changed from foes to friends united in thy service.'"* **(3)**

AND

FOR THE ABILITY TO THINK, READ, AND WRITE, WE SHOULD THANK A TEACHER.

"Those who educate children well are more to be honored than parents, for these gave only life, those the art of living well" (Aristotle on Education).

Chapter One	*Is It Time To Change?*

Before suggesting that any kind of social change is needed, it would be prudent to take a serious look at what we have to work with in terms of our society's moral and social attitude. To do this, some questions need to be asked, such as

> What is important to people today, and how are they responding to what is going on politically, morally, religiously, and financially in their world?

In addition, we need to know to what extent people have accepted the social and moral behavior of today's majority by asking the question:

> At the end of the day, what can you say that you have accomplished which has made your life, your fellow man's life, or your community better?

The answers should give us a feeling for the degree of tolerance one has for the social environment that exists and whether or not they think people today even care about the success of others or if they are even concerned whether decisions have been made with the best interest of the common good.

When you hear about the innocent being murdered in drive-by shootings or a senseless murder of two middle school girlfriends who were shot thirteen times while walking home, it makes you wonder, WHY?

When we hear about senseless crimes like car snatchings, parking lot thefts, and rapes, we wonder what makes people do those things. When we learn about the greed of corporate CEOs who caused their company to file bankruptcy, or hear about a financial planner accused of cheating savings and retirement funds from unsuspecting clients, or trusted government officials who have embezzled thousands of taxpayer funds, we are appalled at the hardship created. Because of all these things that have crippled hundreds of hard working people from having comfortable retirements or a better life, we can conclude that very little attention has been paid to any real commitment to social and moral standards.

All too often, we are reading about stories such as, "Operation Candy Man," a pornography ring organized on the Internet to exploit kids, or stories involving drug use in our schools and the problems young people have experienced because of it. I have to ask, what has happened to the old-fashioned values of honesty, ethics, and morality? Has the covenant given by God to Moses been replaced by one's own version of greed-driven, sinful acts?

I think the ironic thing is while the public is displaying a total indifference to the moral behavior of some of our political leaders and top corporate executives, we have people willing and ready to condemn an entire religion because of the disgraceful actions of a few. Is it because they have developed a "so what" or "as long as it doesn't affect me" type of attitude? Maybe so, but I think our society needs to learn from everyday Christians, like the Love Street Ministries who drive the streets looking for those who need a meal, a coat, or a warm blanket in the winter. This group takes seriously the meaning of the words *ethical, moral, right,* and *wrong.* I have to ask, is our thinking today limited to a "me" venue as opposed to a "we" concept? I think it is important for members of any society to expand and practice those disciplines, which not only help them achieve the goals they want to accomplish for their community, but also helps to make their members more successful citizens.

WHAT DISCIPLINES HAVE WE SEEMED TO HAVE FORGOTTEN ABOUT?

Disciplines, which citizens should regard as essential in order to accomplish any goal, that will benefit them individually and as a society include

1. Mastering those skills that will make one as proficient as possible at his/her life's vocation.

2. Supporting and living by those principles taught by one's chosen theology.

3. Promoting and supporting those life, business, and social decisions that have been morally and ethically conceived for the good of all and not just a few.

4. Working hard to become the person respected and called reliable by friends and associates and recognizing that to become a productive citizen it is important to follow the rules of "law" and fulfill the responsibilities by "choice."

Required by "Law"
- Obey the laws of the land
- Defending our country
- Participate in due process when requested to do so
- Paying the proper amount of taxes
- Acquiring an education

Fulfilled by "Choice"
- Contribute to the common good, such as working to collect food for the poor or contributing proceeds from the sale of donated clothing in order to buy medicine for the poor or elderly
- Holding office
- Participating in election campaigns or voting
- Serving the community—volunteering services
- Participating in a ministry of a selected theology

5. Recognizing that family should be the most important group in your life. You should support them by providing for their safety, welfare, education, and spiritual needs.

6. What is my responsibility to my fellow man, to me, and to God?

7. Will the decision I'm about to make reflect my desire to become more responsible and make it easier for me to make future decisions, or will it make me feel that I can get away with whatever promotes my interest at somebody else's expense?

8. Is what I'm about to do something that I can be proud to say I've done?

9. Are my motives for doing things more for me only, or will they benefit others as well?

10. Does the way I treat others make them feel like I'm a friend, or am I trying to convince them that it is okay to break the rules like others do?

11. Do I consider how my community, the environment, or individual persons will be affected by my decision?

12. Have I asked the questions like, "How will my course of action relate to the moral covenant between my parents and God that I hoped to live by and with the community where I have to live?"

13. What is my responsibility to my fellow man, to me, and to God?

14. What is the bearing of this choice upon my promise of fidelity, self-sacrificial love, care, and service?

15. Will the decision I'm about to make reflect my desire to become more responsible and make it easier for me to make future decisions, or will it make me feel that I can get away with whatever promotes my interest at somebody else's expense?

16. Is what I'm about to do something that I can be proud to say I've done?

17. Are my motives for doing things more for me only, or will they benefit others as well?

18. Does the way I treat others make them feel like I'm a friend, or am I trying to convinced them that it is okay to break the rules like others do?

19. Do I consider how my community, the environment, or individual persons will be affected by my decision?

20. Have you considered what responsibilities you must accept in presenting, promoting, and what you must do toward its implementation?

IN THE BEGINNING: God said man should have a woman to live with as one flesh, faithful to each other and reproduce. This command requires special obligations on both man and woman as well as emphasizes the need for society to promote and work for the success of the common good. Individuals who respect one another and work harmoniously usually accomplish their goals. It is the family that is God's way of giving us an extra incentive to work together and to acquire respect for the rights and contributions of others. When we understand that it is the preservation of the family and the freedom to love God that becomes the principal purpose for defending our rights, inherited freedoms, and the opportunity to create a peaceful and loving future for all, then we fully understand the need for us to fulfill our civic and spiritual duties. It is within these two boundaries that are our largest responsibilities lie. For example:

1. To perform our civic duties, we are required to
   a. promote the common good by being charitable,
   b. promote integrity,
   c. vote,
   d. work to eliminate deceit and misuse of public funds,
   e. promote healthy recreational activities, modern educational opportunities, sponsor cultural activities, and provide health and welfare programs and services,
   f. provide police and fire protection and maintain a safe infrastructure.

2. Our spiritual duties require us
   a. to promote the common good. To help in this process, we should use our talents when and where needed by participating in community-sponsored programs and projects.
   b. We should be active in church, mosque, or synagogue activities, work to support social goals and projects, and participate in and promote educational and social ministry programs.

I have often wondered, how do we get people in the pew on Sunday to act like God's disciples on Monday through Saturday? Too often, we see a very humble attitude on Sunday but a different one on Monday. One of God's expectations is that we "work at it," a human activity not seemingly cherished by many.

IS IT DOABLE? The degree of competence and success in accomplishing these goals will vary according to each individual's academic and social accomplishments, it is true; but in my opinion, it is the disciplines of **morality, ethics, education, and religious participation** within a society that makes up the prevailing attitudes and behavior within that society. These are the ingredients, along with an effective oral and written communications ability, that serves as the nucleus for accomplishing the task of becoming a more effective citizen. These values are reflective in an individual's everyday decisions and contribute greatly to the growth and development of one's personal and Christian success; therefore, I have placed a great deal of emphasis on their importance and the importance of raising the reader's proficiency in using them in this presentation.

One of the first things needed to determine if change is needed is to examine the prevailing philosophy that exists in our society. To change a society requires moral maturity, which means we need to make choosing the common good a matter of desire and routine habit. To do this will require some changes in attitude among those who have become known as representing the traditionalists' image of society. Most of us have very little opportunity to define our own projects and agendas because the overall structure of social life is pre-established for the most part by others and even enforced in most cases by the elites. Individuals must "fit in," if you will. Knowing who we are, what we need to do, and how we think, combined with an honest admission that we do not already know the answer to what our choices should be, are very important steps in making a commitment to accomplishing moral deliberation, finding compromises, and feeling the need to share all ideas before reaching conclusions. Faith is also required to be a part of our decision process. When we are constantly affirming our trust in God, our confidence in Him becomes stronger and more apparent to others. It also makes it easier to continue the task of trying to develop moral and ethical meaning to our decisions. While it is true that Christian faith is difficult to teach, it can, by individual example, be ever present in our actions and play a huge role in our becoming a person to trust.

DO WE THINK CHANGES ARE NEEDED TODAY? POLITICS AND CHANGE: There is probably no better time to ask questions dealing with the need for change in our society than during a presidential campaign. All the candidates can tell us is that our country is in a mess. They cite everything from government overspending to the increasing cost of goods and services and the war, which has been a financial burden as well as a tragedy, in terms of the lost of human life and the disruption it has caused to a cultural many centuries old. Those with opposing solutions, who are running for office, simply say what they think their local voters want to hear. Around the globe, countries are being invaded, banks are in a mess, home mortgage lenders are foreclosing at a rate never seen before, banks are not granting loans, businesses cannot get loans to meet payroll, expand, hire new employees, do research, etc., the automakers may be forced into bankruptcy. The interesting thing, according to the left-wing informational sources this was all caused by one man. RIGHT!

JUST LOOK AROUND AT OUR BEHAVIOR

FOR THE SAKE OF OIL: Recently, the Soviet Union invaded the small country of Georgia, which was formerly under the rule of the Soviet Union before their breakup. Georgia is a Christian state with a democratic form of government and a president elected by the people. Russia wants to take over and occupy this little country. Maybe oil and gas could be the reason!

Dr. Ariel Cohen in an article entitled, "The Russian-Georgian War: A Challenge for the U.S. and the World," published by the Heritage Foundation shortly after Russia's invasion of Georgia in August of 2008 offers his reasons for Russia's invasion. Dr. Cohen says, "Russia's goals for the war with Georgia are far-reaching and include:

> . . . Expulsion of Georgian troops and termination of Georgian sovereignty in South Ossetia and Abkhazia

... "Regime change" by bringing down President Mikheil
Saakashvilli and installing a more pro-Russian leadership
in Tbillisi;

... Preventing Georgia from joining NATO and sending a
strong message to Ukraine that its insistence on NATO
membership may lead to war and or its dismemberment;

... Shifting control of the Caucasus, and especially over
strategic energy pipelines, by controlling Georgia; and

... Recreating a 19th century-style sphere of influence in the
former Soviet Union, by the use of force if necessary.

Russia is demonstrating that it can sabotage American and European
Union declarations about integrating Commonwealth of Independent
States members into Western structures such as NATO. By attempting
to accomplish a regime change in Georgia, Moscow is also trying to
gain control of the energy and transportation corridor, which connects
Central Asia and Azerbaijan with the Black Sea and ocean routes overseas
for oil, gas, and other commodities. A pro-Russian regime in Georgia
will also bring the strategic Baku-Tbilisi-Ceyhan oil pipeline and the
Baku-Erzurum (Turkey) gas pipeline under Moscow's control. Such a
development would undermine any options of pro-Western orientation
for Azerbaijan and Armenia, along with any chances of resolving their
conflict based on diplomacy and Western-style cooperation.

Dr. Cohen continues to write that the United States and its European
allies must take all available diplomatic measures to stop Russian
aggression. The United States and its allies need to demand that Russia
withdraw all its troops from the territory of Georgia and recognize its
territorial integrity. Furthermore, the United States and Europe need to
internationalize the conflict. Russian desire to be viewed as upholder of
international law needs to be turned against Moscow. The Organization
for Security and Cooperation in Europe (OSCE), the EU and the United
Nations should send other international observers to Georgia while
mediation efforts to withdraw Russian forces need to be expedited. The
United States, its allies, and other countries need to send a strong signal
to Moscow that creating nineteenth century-style spheres of influence

and redrawing the borders of the former Soviet Union is a danger to world peace. Moscow's plan cannot be accomplished without violation of international law and is likely to result in death and destruction—a price that neither the Russian people nor the other should pay." **(1)**

Activity such as this could lead to another downfall of the Soviet Union when we consider their former attitudes concerning their behavior toward other countries in the world. The behavior of the old Russia can be typified by some of its more colorful leaders. Some of you might remember Nikita Khrushchev who became premier of the Soviet Union in 1958. Khrushchev sought to lower the burden of defense spending on the Soviet economy by placing a new emphasis on rocket-based defense. The Soviet lead in this technology was emphasized by the success of Sputnik 1 and subsequently Yuri Gagarin's Vostok flight in space. Sputnik's success was the inspiration for the movie *October Sky*, which is showed in most of our high school science classes today. During the '60s, the fear of the success of the Soviet missile forces became a concern for the West and was a subject of debate in the 1960 presidential campaign when candidate Senator John F. Kennedy attacked then—vice president Richard M. Nixon over the missile gap. When Kennedy became president, the Soviets soon tested the president by creating the Cuban missile crisis. Yours truly was standing ready in Germany, with a rifle loaded, waiting to see whether or not WW III was about to begin. Another act of aggression, which showed very little concern for its citizens, occurred in 1961 when Khrushchev approved plans proposed by Communist East German leader Walter Ulbricht to build the Berlin Wall, which would separate the Communist East from the free West.

Khrushchev was known for making blunders. He had very poor diplomatic skills, giving him the reputation of being a rude, uncivilized peasant in the West and as an irresponsible clown in his own country. This was probably due to his lack of formal education. His lack of morality, integrity, and respect for human rights was also emphasized by his lack of respect for the principles of the Russian church. Khrushchev renewed persecutions against the Russian Orthodox Church, publicly promising to show the "last priest" on Soviet television. Between 1960 and 1962, as many as 30 percent of the churches were destroyed with the number of monasteries falling by a quarter. He was constantly disrupting the proceedings in the United Nations General Assembly between September and October

1960 by pounding his fists on the desk and shouting in Russian. He twice interrupted the British Prime Minister Harold Macmillan, and some of us will recall the notorious shoe-banging incident, which occurred during a debate over a Russian resolution decrying colonialism. He accused the Filipino delegate Lorenzo Sumulong of being "a jerk, a stooge and a lackey of imperialism." Later on in his career, Khrushchev said, in reference to capitalism at a United Nation's meeting, "We will bury you." This caused a tremendous amount of contempt for the premier that he later said, "I once got in trouble for saying, 'We will bury you.' Of course, we will not bury you with a shovel. Your own working class will bury you." His administration, although efficient, disbanded a large number of Stalinist-era agencies that tended to make it somewhat erratic. He took a dangerous gamble in 1962 over Cuba, which took the superpowers to the brink of a third World War. Agriculture barely kept up with population growth as bad harvests mixed with good ones, culminating in a disastrous harvest in 1963 due to the weather. Just like he had acted, his downfall came as a result of a conspiracy among the party bosses, who were irritated by his erratic policies and cantankerous behavior. The conspirators struck in October 1964, when Khrushchev was on vacation. They called a special meeting of the Central Committee, Khrushchev's critical base of support, to take action against him. He resigned as the premier of the Soviet Union on October 15, 1964. **(2)**

Mikhail Gorbachev, who became the Soviet Union's leader in 1985, was inspired by Khrushchev's de-Stalinization philosophy of encouraging more liberal communist leaders to replace hard-line Stalinists throughout the Eastern bloc as was evidenced by his policies of glasnost and perestroika. In 1987, however, Gorbachev was challenge by the United State's President Ronald Reagan to destroy the Berlin Wall, which had been built by the Communist East Germans. Arriving in Berlin on June 12, 1987, President Reagan and Mrs. Regan were taken to the Reichstag, where they viewed the wall from a balcony. Reagan made his speech at the Brandenburg Gate at 2:00 PM in front of two panes of bulletproof glass protecting him from potential snipers in East Berlin. President Reagan said:

> We welcome change and openness; for we believe that freedom
> and security go together, that the advance of human liberty
> can only strengthen the cause of world peace. There is one

sign the Soviets can make that would be unmistakable, that would advance dramatically the cause of freedom and peace. General Secretary Gorbachev, if you seek peace, if you seek prosperity for the Soviet Union and eastern Europe, if you seek liberalization, come here to this gate. Mr. Gorbachev, open this gate. Mr. Gorbachev, tear down this wall!

Another highlight of the speech was Reagan's call to end the arms race with his reference to the Soviets' SS-20 nuclear weapons, and possibility of "not merely of limiting the growth of arms, but of eliminating, for the first time, an entire class of nuclear weapons from the face of the Earth." Twenty-nine months later, Gorbachev allowed Berliners to destroy the wall, and the Soviet Union collapsed soon afterward. **(3)**

This leader of a major European country, who was willing to create conspiracies against his own party bosses and called by his politburo a harebrained schemer of erratic policies, was constantly an embarrassment to the Soviets by constantly humiliating the ruling elite with his social blunders. Gorbachev lacked knowledge and understanding of the world outside of his direct experience and often proved easy to be manipulated by hucksters who knew how to appeal to his vanity and prejudices. He was a name caller, rude, and totally arrogant. With this background, is it any wonder the Russians invaded Georgia and now are planning ways of once again desirous of the Ukraine to be once again under their rule? **(4)**

DO WE WELCOME THEM OR TREAT THEM AS UNWELCOMED GUESTS? ARE THEY CALLED IMMIGRANTS OR INVADERS?

In communities with a large population of Hispanics you'll hear, "something needs to be done about illegal immigration." I'm not for breaking the law, but I'm for anyone who is willing to sacrifice their life for an opportunity to live in a better place. The Mexicans, in my area of the world, are hardworking, good people. I'm sure they would rather live in their own native country, but their government chooses not to provide them opportunities to earn a decent wage or to allow them to afford adequate housing. Therefore, they leave their homeland at the risk of dying in order to provide their family with a decent life. What needs to be done is to change the immigration laws and make it possible for honest people to live in a free country and raise their family with a proud sense of accomplishment. Remember the discrimination felt by Native Americans over the years, the hardships suffered by black Africans who were brought from Africa to be slaves, the Civil War—the most costly war in terms of the loss of human life, which was supposed to win blacks their independence. Remember the Chinese who, along with the Irish, built the railroads and especially the born-in-America Japanese who were treated like the enemy and were imprisoned during World War II? Did you forget that most of the western half of Texas—all of New Mexico, Arizona, and Southern California—belonged to the Mexicans as early as the 1850s? Mexicans, like Native Americans, were cheated out of their land by slick treaties and promises made in good faith. Remember the Treaty of Guadalupe Hidalgo or the stories told by Black Elk? Well you should! Maybe it would be well to reread our history books and think about what conclusions you would have made under the same circumstances.

Other subjects concern the American people during presidential campaigns such as the high cost of goods and services, especially the higher cost of food and gasoline. Taxes are too high and the difficulty to acquire loans are prohibiting people the right to own property. Banks are in terrible shape partly because Fannie Mae and Freddie Mac are not working. Financial institutions have had to be bailed out to the tune of $250,000,000 to start over because of greedy lending practices. People are defaulting on their creative mortgages these institutions saddled them with because the value of their houses have decreased while payments under interest only mortgages and variable rate mortgages have increased. Many have lost their jobs due to downsizing, mergers, and their employers' inability to get loans to cover payroll, buy supplies, marketing, and transportation costs.

A recent report by pollingreport.com for the CNN Web site, CNNPolitics. com, cited their list of the most important issues concerning registered voters as being the economy, followed by the war in Iraq, health care, terrorism, and immigration. Other concerns included abortion, Afghanistan, the environment, social security, stem cell research, guns, free trade, and Iran. It's amazing how wrong things can become in four to eight years. Who gets the blame? It seems people are more interest in blaming the president and his administration and not Congress who make the laws and support the president's decision to declare war or the Senate who spends the money. People should work hard to change those laws and procedures that cause these problems by becoming more involved in supporting those that will work to change things in favor of supporting and working to implement laws that will help the common good now and in the future.

DID YOU EVER HEAR ABOUT THE UAW?

I received an e-mail from a classmate of my wife regarding the plight of the auto business.

Subject: compensation packages of Detroit Auto Workers, this is incredible. According to Forbes magazine the Labor cost per hour, wages and benefits for hourly workers are as follows:

Ford:	$70.51 per hour	($141,020. per year)
General Motors:	$73.26 per hour	($146,520. per year)
Chrysler:	$75.86 per hour	($151,720. per year)
Toyota, Honda, Nissan (in US)	$48.00 per hour	($ 73,207. per year)

According to AAUP (the American Association of University Professors), the average annual compensation for a college professor in 2006 was $92,973. (Average salary nationally of $73,207 + 27 percent in benefits). The bottom line is that the average USW worker with a high school diploma ears 57.6 percent more compensation than the average university professor with a PhD, and 52.6 percent more than the average worker at Toyota, Honda, or Nissan. Many industry analysts say the Detroit Three must be on par with Toyota and Honda to survive. This year's contract must be "transformational" in reducing pension and health care costs. What does "transformational" mean? One way to think about "transformational" would mean that UAW workers, most with a high school diploma, would have to accept compensation equal to that of the average university professor with a PhD.

Then there is the "job bank" when a Detroit Three lays an employee off, that employee continues to receive all benefits, medical, retirement, etc., plus an hourly wage of $31 per hour. Here's a typical story, writes my friend. Ken Pool is making good money. On weekdays, he shows up at

8:00 a.m. at Ford Motor Co.'s Michigan Truck Plant in Wayne, signs in, and then starts working on a crossword puzzle. Pool hates the monotony, but the pay is good: more than $31.00 an hour plus benefits. "We just go in and play crossword puzzles, watch videos that someone brings in or read the newspaper," he says. "Otherwise, I just sit."

Pool is one of more than 12,000 American autoworkers who, instead of installing windshields or bending sheet metal, spend their days counting the hours in a jobs bank set up by Detroit automakers as demanded by the United Auto Workers Union (UAW) as part of an extraordinary job security agreement. Now the Detroit Three wants Joe Taxpayer to pick up this tab in a $25 billion bailout package, which is soon to be increased to $45 billion if our government leaders in congress and some senators have their way. The Detroit Three want this money, not to build better cars but to pay the tab for medical and retirement benefits for retired autoworkers. Not one penny would be used to make them more competitive or to improve the quality of their cars. We all have problems paying for our medical insurance, but the political leaders in Congress now want us to pay the medical insurance premiums of folks who have retired from Ford, GM, and Chrysler. HOW ABOUT CHAPTER 11 and getting rid of these ridiculous union contracts? Where do you think the autoworkers stand on this issue, and what does this have to do with Joe and Mary's mortgage they are struggling to pay? Where can it end? **(5)**

NEVER COMPROMISE YOUR VALUES: Some time ago, I received a letter regarding a new group that was in the process of organizing a faith-based coalition to deal with various community issues. The group being formed was going to be a metropolitan area interfaith committee made up of several churches in the metropolitan area. The purpose was for them to join together to discuss ways to more effectively address the pressures facing families in the community.

The letter said that the group was started in 2007 and had now become convinced that the time was right for establishing a Congregational Based Community Organizing (CBCO), a group that would provide congregations with the tools they needed to better understand the pressures facing families; to more consistently identify and train potential leaders within the congregation; to make more explicit the connection between faith, worship, and life; to work with other institutions, including public schools and civic groups; and to learn to use the democratic process effectively so that families can have a voice in what happens to their neighborhoods, schools, and the greater community. Because a small number of people do not have the power needed to truly infleunce the policies and actions of local public officials like larger numbers, the game plan made sense.

To get things started, each church's congregation, wishing to participate, would hold house meetings with interested participants to discuss the problems facing the families of their congregations. Group leaders would then bring a list of concerns to the total congregation who would select one or two issues to bring to the attention of participants who attended the larger metro meeting. At the metro meeting, those issues that reflected the most common concerns of the congregations from the community would be selected as long as the issues did not conflict with any one church's social teachings. We sometimes focus so much on charity that we leave little time to think about justice, they said.

The letter went on to say, in order to make the effort successful, the organization would need professional leadership experience and the group known as the IAF would provide everything needed to include: leadership training in both congregational development and public action as institutions work together to reflect on their own religious and spiritual teachings that relate to developing a community that practices solidarity, to hear the stories of individuals and families as they face pressures in the larger community and help them to focus on a specific concern and formalize an agenda or statement of the issues within each faith community individually, to create a citywide agenda based on issues of common concern, and to enter into research and agreed-upon actions that will improve the lives of individuals and families by holding public officials accountable to the needs of families. Does this sound like something that could benefit the common good? **(6)**

The ideal utopia was Christians, Jews, Muslims, Hindus, Buddhists, and members of all other religions would be learning from each other and would be forming issues that concerned all of them. As a group, these issues would be brought to the respective political entity for resolution or further discussion. In my city, approximately twenty-five churches joined in a metropolitan organization. They included Catholics, Methodists, Presbyterians, Nazarenes, Unitarians, Baptists, and the United Church of Christ members. To pay for this leadership, the IAF would charge each member group between $1,500 and $7,500 per year. The IAF would be responsible for deciding the common issues to be included in the metrowide agenda. Since the agenda could not violate anyone's religious teachings or traditions, Catholics for example could not take on issues such as abortion or gay issues since those went against their social justice teaching. Herein lies the problem. If a Catholic parish wanted to pursue a project that supported traditional marriage or was pro-life, the IAF leader would explain that such projects were too divisive and that we must select a project that is acceptable to the non-Catholic churches in the larger community program. They would insist that the consensus was more important that anyone's particular issue.

All of us belong to the largest community organization in the world called the "one holy, catholic and apostolic church." We can all do better for the common good by pursuing the social injustices that supports our faith as opposed to a group that proudly say they are openly radical and continue to practice what their founding fathers, Saul Alinsky and his successor Edward T. Chambers, preached, which was radicalism. These men were political activist. In his book, *Rules for Radicals*, Alinsky begins with a tribute to the one he admired most. He wrote, "From all our legends, mythology, and history (and who is to know where mythology leaves off and history begins—or which is which), the first radical known to man who rebelled against the establishment and did it so effectively that he at least won his own kingdom—Lucifer." We do not need this kind of leadership.

CAN THE PRESIDENT SOLVE OUR PROBLEMS?
No man or woman has ever been more scrutinized than a candidate to become president of the United States of America. This position has to be one of the toughest jobs a person could have. One needs to know everything there is to know and have the answers to all questions on every subject that can be asked and to the satisfaction of the majority of voters and the media. He/she must remember what was said years ago, on all subjects, to whom it was said, what the response was, and what one's opponent said and did since he/she came out of the cradle. Any vote that was ever casted needs to be defended, every church service

one attended needs to be reviewed, every friend or relative that ever said howdy or made an off-key comment or referred to any racial matters will set you behind in the polls for a long time. The money it takes to run a campaign could provide a lot of food, supplies, and services for those who really need the help the most.

The interesting thing is how the media responds to all this. They try to elect their candidate on his party affiliation and what they anticipate will be the candidate's methods for solving the problems and not on the person's character, integrity, moral behavior, or concern for the welfare of the common good. A presidential candidate must promise every cure for every ill the voters want, knowing for certain that he would have to be Santa Claus, Jesus, the Easter Bunny, the Good Fairy, and the Wizard of Oz all rolled into one to be able to produce all that is promised. The irony is that the American people base their support on the amount and type of promises made. "What's in it for me" is the battle cry as if people all over these fifty states do not have the same concerns and the opportunity to earn a decent living, buy a home, provide for their family, send their kids off to college.

Election issues are usually the same every four years, but the candidates themselves usually have different agendas as to why they want to be elected to the highest office in the land. Could any one person possess all these attributes? No, and they know it. During a campaign, it takes thousands of staffers to supply answers to the anticipated questions the candidate must face. Staffers must analyze what voter attitudes are on various subjects. Questions and their answers, as well as voter concerns, are different in each geographic location. In order to provide the answers voters want to hear requires huge amounts of research and a mountain of promises, which will cover all the concerns of the voters. Candidates present their solutions by making promises they know they cannot fulfill but are solutions that the voters want to hear. The 2008 campaign started months before usual, and candidates were elected by unanimous consent for the first time that I can remember at their respective party conventions. Voters have legitimate concerns, and the economy is borderline to the tragedies that were created by the great depression. People have lost millions of retirement dollars because of the public's reaction to the troubles in our economy, but instead of selecting the candidate they think will work to produce the kinds of solutions that will convince congress and the senate to implement those policies that will work to improve the situations which caused the problem, they vote on the basis of what the prior party didn't accomplish to solve the problems and their fairy tale promises. Congressmen and senators make decisions, the administration has other responsibilities, so if you do not like what's going on, write, call, meet with, and lobby your congressman or senator who is suppose to represent you and not the lobbyist. The gay's and the lesbians have. The pro-life people have.

Ask your congressman why it takes a concentration on pork in otherwise important legislation to get anything done for your state. If congresmen and senators see that the public is upset with them as opposed to blaming the administration for all their problems, something may be done. But then, there is the almighty press, TV, and talk show philosophers that help us make up our mind when it should be our minds which are being made up to get rid of those who are not working in the best interest of the common good.

The proven moral character and integrity of presidential candidates seem to be less important than their created empty promises. Whether or not the candidate has had a hand in directing military forces, knows what it takes to meet a payroll, or promotes life instead of death to the unborn, seems less important than making promises that will never be fulfilled. We need to have faith in the candidate we vote for; therefore, he or she has to have done something to show that their promises and plans can be obtained and not wished. We need to believe, regardless of party affiliation, that the candidate we choose has the experience, credentials, and the ability to create an atmosphere of cooperation within the congress and senate to pass the laws and spend money for positive solutions for the good of our country and not just their state. The president should have a strong desire to protect our borders, an ability to mandate the compliance of contracts and laws, and possess the character to act in a responsible way when we are threaten by outside forces that want to harm us whether it be economically or by force.

The character of the president should include respect for human life, a belief in providing citizens the opportunity to earn a respectable living, provide the opportunity to own property, support human life, and maintain an adequate staff to see that the branches of government run efficiently and are financially prudent. The president needs to provide the watchdogs to watch over those corporate entities and their CEOs that would break the laws of the land in favor of their own greed, ambitions, and desires. In essence, since we are asked to have faith in a leader that is commissioned with the responsibility to help our country maintain the moral and ethical character it has always enjoyed, we should pray that we make the right decision in selecting that leader who will fulfill those requirements. We pray to God to help us with our personal needs, to watch over the sick, and a variety of other things. Why not ask him to help us vote for a leader who will do the best job possible for the good of our country, our allies, and the people of the world. and when elected, continue to pray that God will guide him, give him the character to do what is best for the country, while providing for the protection of our dignity and freedom?

WHAT ABOUT MORAL ISSUES: San Francisco has now joined Massachusetts as the only other state that recognizes same-sex marriages. CNN's Web site, Politics.com reported, "Issues that affect the lesbian, gay, bisexual and transgender (LGBT) community look to play a prominent role in this year's presidential campaign." **(7)** Although we haven't had any sex in the oval office lately or representatives running away with those who work for them, we do seem to have a huge tolerance for individuals who want to choose their way instead of the acceptable moral majority way. On that subject, I will let God decide how to handle the controversy they are experiencing; as for me, I'm glad I have a loving wife and great kids to share life's pleasures. The war is a moral thing causing mixed emotions. One party wants us out in X amount of months regardless of the stability of the country while the other wants to get out after victory has been declared and the country is able to conduct its business in peace. Do these people not know that we still have U.S. soldiers in places such as Germany, Korea, and Japan? Some are even being killed, not with enemy bullets but because of things like ongoing training accidents, natural causes, unavoidable accidents, and bad judgment while on leave. How quickly would you want someone who is trying to help you to be able to live in a free society, allow women and all children the opportunity to go to school to become whatever their talents will allow, go away because there is a price to pay for freedom, a price to pay for a better life no matter how it is defined? Should we say, "Good luck with that" and leave? "I have to go because people in

America don't want you to have the same privileges they have in their country, and we have our problems too." Where would you find this type of attitude and behavior in the Bible, in U.S. history? Do you realize we killed over 600,000 Americans over slavery in our country during the Civil War? How moral is that?

On the youth scene today, more and more young people have alcohol—and drug-related addictions. Schools have to battle the behavior of those under the influence every day. According to WebMD, "10% of teens smoke cigarettes, 75% of high school students have tried alcohol, 40% of teens have tried marijuana one or more times, and 9% of teens have tried cocaine, while 4% use it currently one or more times in a month." Teens also inhale glues, aerosol sprays, gasoline, paints, and paint thinners. Other drugs that have been used for immoral purposes include the club drugs, which includes ecstasy and date rape drugs. Drugs referred to as meth, crack, or speed, hallucinogens, opiates—such as heroin, morphine, and codeine—can lead to strong physical and psychological addiction. Teens who use addictive drugs like these may steal, prostitute themselves, or resort to other dangerous or illegal behavior to buy drugs. Also being used are cough syrups and cold pills, prescription drugs both from the medicine cabinet at home, vodka, gin, and whiskey from the bar at home, and anabolic steroids from who knows were. What type of citizens will this behavior produce? The American Academy of Child and Adolescent Psychiatry reports each year more than 10,000 young people in the United States are killed and 40,000 injured in alcohol-related automobile accidents. Their updated May 2008 report showed experimentation with alcohol and drugs during adolescence is common. Teenagers at risk for developing serious alcohol and drug problems include those

- with a family history of substance abuse,
- who are depressed,
- who have low self-esteem, and
- who feel like they don't fit in or are out of the mainstream.

Warning signs according to the Academy report includes

Physical: Fatigue, repeated health complaints, red and glazed eyes, and a lasting cough.

Emotional: personality change, sudden mood changes, irritability, irresponsible behavior, low self-esteem, poor judgment, depression, and a general lack of interest.

Family: starting arguments, breaking rules, or withdrawing from the family. **(8)**

Educationally, a lot of changes need to be made, but we can't help children learn if they are not attending school. A recent article in my local paper, regarding the truancy of our public school students quoted researchers with the National Center for Poverty at Columbia University, Children in Poverty, who found that one in ten kindergarten and first-grade students miss what amounts to at least a month of school between excused and unexcused absences during the school year. These researchers found that children from poor families are most at risk calling their discovery as "remarkable as it is consequential." The opinion goes on to say that "schools and communities have a choice: We can work together early on to ensure families get their children to class consistently or we can pay later for failing to intervene before problems are more difficult and costly to ameliorate." **(9)**

There have been many comments made by colleges all over the country that high school graduates are not prepared to do college work. From the Web site of the Chicago Tribune comes a story that reveals what parents and students will do to be considered over their rivals for admission to the more selective colleges. Because of the competition, parents and their student applicants are writing letters to the college admissions offices suggesting that rival applicants have participated in social decisions not becoming to the behavior of their university's standards, such as "the applicant cheated on exams or got suspended for underage drinking." Sometimes, according to the article, they include an unflattering newspaper clipping or a sly suggestion to check our pictures of a student's Facebook page. **(10)** With this kind of behavior, no wonder students have such an alarming dropout rate.

When faced with the decision to make a choice, people unfortunately focus on the question, "What's in it for me?" For some, the ability to make choices are limited by a person's ability to think, which is something that's not on every teacher's priority list of things to teach in our public schools these days. For various reasons, preparing and taking tests are more important than the time it takes to teach a student how to think. Unfortunately, life after school bells will require us to think and make good choices in order to survive with a minimum of bumps and bruises on the road toward life's end. What might save us is the degree of knowledge acquired during our life experiences and what these experiences have taught us. The amount of formal education we have been able to complete, combined with our life's experiences, should give us a better chance at becoming a person who can recognize what is required to make things better. Our experiences and formal education may give us the ability to focus on the problems we face and the ability to make better choices. The outcome will of course depend on how well these two realities, experience and education, have been absorbed. If we have learned well, they may also teach us how to factor in to the equation some degree of common sense, which is a discipline also often overlooked on the list of things to emphasize or talk about with young people.

We know that epistemology is the investigation into the grounds and nature of knowledge itself and have concluded that it is these two terms (*experience* and *education*) that defines the necessary ingredients needed in order to fundamentally know how to think. Since it is knowledge and experience that creates limitations on our ability to develop moral and ethical standards, it should follow that if we don't know anything about the environment we're in or do not know by reason of experience or formal education what complements the situation we are faced with, it stands to reason that we cannot be expected to know how to respond. Therefore, we only need to acknowledge knowing what our responsibilities are in any given situation based on what we have learned by experience and education. It is our responsibility, however, to constantly learn how to apply our experiences and education to problems we have not experienced before and how to analyze the problem, explore the facts, ask questions, and experiment with solutions. Our ability to reason things successfully will eventually become more efficient and make us better able to reach conclusions that will better serve our needs. If we can discipline ourselves to turn to history, literature, and the Bible, what we have not learned from our formal education or experience can often be found in these sources.

Following the path of our educational pursuits and the experiences we have had leads us somewhere between the culture level we are now and the outer limits of our knowledge; therein lies our visual, moral, and ethical horizons. From this point of view, what we value, care about, and what we think, is developed. Our attitudes, goals, and beliefs sometimes try to stretch beyond these limitations but only knowledge can answer "fact" questions and restrict our behavior. By taking proper responsibility for our actions, which have been generated from our knowledge, we create a strategy for acknowledging how our acts of moral understanding, judgment, and decisions will be structured. This act creates a routine or thought process in us, which focuses on how we recognize one's ability. In order to know what motivates people, we need to analyze their performance during the course of their daily routines. By experiencing, judging, and deciding the results of their performance, we can tell whether or not—according to their environment—their behavior is right or wrong according to our known acceptable standards. Creating such a thought process establishes an appreciation for the moral and ethical behavior expected by a more sophisticated society or a different cultural.

We seem to experience a degree of shyness the bigger the world becomes because we feel less confident that we can predict whether our behavior will be right or wrong. To be moral and ethical, then, refers to any experience in our life that causes us to first consider who the problem affects, the ability to create a plan that will help that person or group before formulating a plan on how to proceed to implement those solutions that will help the most people. To be morally and ethically correct assumes that an acknowledgment of the problems are necessary in order to understand what the needs of the people involved are before any proposed solutions to solve the problem can be made and what long-term requirements and commitments to maintain the solutions will be necessary to maintain those solutions if implemented. Suggestions need to be made with the best interest of the common good and should be flexible enough to meet future changing societal conditions. It is therefore our actions, which cause us to achieve objectives and goals, which in turn makes moral knowledge a skill that must be learned.

Solutions require cooperation: In the process of implementing any solutions, cooperation, rather than conflict, needs to be the foundation for any social order whether it is a large society or a small one. Classes and cultures should be aware that it takes the wealthy as well as the working class in order to reach a working harmony. Each group must show respect for the responsibilities each must fulfill. When different classes and cultures maintain a cooperative, rather than a resentful demeanor, more can be accomplished and the proper groundwork can be laid for a better economy to emerge. This blending of cultures and classes provides the experiences for all to grow. Pope Leo XIII addressed, as far back as 1891, in his encyclical "Rerum Novarum" what he saw as a major societal problem, which brought this point home to both the upper and working classes. The rights of workers needed to be protected, he said, and the wealth of a society needs to be shared so that all the wealth is not limited to a few, which would give the wealthy the power to maintain undue political power for the benefit of a few. Pope Leo suggested that making property available to the working class and promoting workers to join the unions and take a more active role in the churches who could influence them would serve to accomplish both concerns. He reasoned that it was ownership in property or wealth that tended to soothe the hurt of a chaotic society and what better would call on the sinful of all classes to take inventory of their life than the church.

It seems to me if we ask ourselves the question, "What can I do to make this a better world and to make me a better citizen?" we will usually turn to that which makes us think about and examine our life from a theological point of view to find answers. The only place short of looking down the barrel of a 12-gauge shotgun that makes us reflect seriously about our life or look in the mirror to discern consequences of our actions are our churches, mosques, temples, and synagogues. The problem with Leo's suggestion was, if the church was to be a private institution dedicated to all who sought the truth, how does the church use its influence to change the thinking of its class-structured society? Pope Leo's response suggested that the answer should be centered on the teaching and universal philosophy of Jesus's teaching.

Motivational and educationally inspired theological messages bring to light an awareness of our moral and ethical obligation to support and promote the principles of peace, love, respect, compassion, and charity. Rich or poor, we have the same responsibility to our fellow man, which is to promote justice, respect, and make choices that support the best interest of the common good. Knowledge can produce influential powers as well as the politically favored; and when an atmosphere of cooperation is established and all talents are working together, solutions are more likely to be reached, which are mutually acceptable to all parties. The threads that bind our moral code of conduct to our actions are our knowledge, ability to reason, and our life's experiences. Therefore, we reach out to the only solution available to us, as did Pope Leo in 1891, to our house of worship. Here, all are welcome, all are classless, and all have the same objective, which is to hear and learn the word and lessons of God.

If we are humble on Sunday and take to heart all that is taught in the gospel, why can't we take our God-given talent, each with their own specialty and influence, to do what's right for the good of man on Monday? Perhaps we do not let our personal experience play its proper role in the development of our faith. Our experiences create images, which in turn brings insight, awareness, and finally action; but when we operate exclusively from a standpoint of certitude, we are unable to test a new experience against the view of life that we hold. What happens is our current interpretations become absolute, unchanging, and true. It is important to remember that Jesus gave us forgiveness for our sins and ultimately the power to respond to new possibilities.

As the author of Hebrews writes, "Faith is the realization of what is hoped for and evidence of things not seen" (Heb. 11:1). What this means is that we can therefore believe, by having faith, the best is yet to come. The study of God (theology) is a faith-seeking understanding. The study of God becomes the process, which blossoms into your beliefs, the product. Why does God let man forsake him? God created a challenge to the prophet. He used him to vent his dissatisfaction. The prophet's greatest concern is much like that of God's, "What is man's future going to be?" Why is man so rebellious when he knows that God is so saddened when man forsakes Him? God gave us the freedom to make choices; maybe God is saddened that the freedom of man to make his own choice wasn't such a good idea. But on the other hand, if we believe that nothing can stop God from offering salvation to every human being, why do we need to make excuses for not doing his will?

Is it time to make some changes? YES

Think About It:

Proverbs 11:29 (the New Jerusalem Bible) says, "Whoever misgoverns a house inherits the wind, and the fool becomes slave to the wise."

THINGS WE SHOULD ALL THINK ABOUT

Bernard Lonergan, in his work *Method in Theology* observed that the ideal basis for a society is the community it develops. Likewise, the community must take its stand on a moral, a religious, or a Christian principle. The moral principle is that men individually are responsible for what they make of themselves but collectively they are responsible for the world in which they live. Such is the basis for universal dialogue. The religious principle is God's gift of his love, which forms the basis of a dialogue between all representatives of religion. The Christian principle conjoins the inner gift of God's love with its outer manifestation in Christ Jesus and in those who follow him. Such is the basis of Christian ecumenism, according to Lonergan.

We, as a community, seem to make things more complicated than it needs to be. I suppose the influence created by the existence of a multicultural thought process is what lends itself to disagreements and is what is responsible for the attitude of a cooperative standoff. When God, speaking through the prophets of the Old Testament realized that he had given them an almost impossible task to accomplish, he decided to give his people one more chance. "The word made flesh."

If I were a prophet in today's world, I would be primarily concerned with ethics and our lack of commitment to social and moral responsibilities. I am particularly astonished by the lack of integrity that seems to prevail in the business environment, and especially, I am appalled with the public's indifference to the moral behavior of our political leaders and representatives. In today's world, it is unfortunate, but I would have a wealth of ethical issues to attack, i.e., conflict of interest issues in business, law, and medicine, scandals in government, sexual harassment in the workplace, charges of misappropriation of public funds, women's rights, and the perennial clashes among interest groups over issues of environment, homosexuality, abortion, euthanasia, genetic engineering, pornography, health care, education, and the future of our social services. The list goes on. While ethics and morality seem to be in the forefront of public attention, public agreement on how to approach the problems seems to have reached an all-time low. When one gives a reason for their concern, invariably, a debate over the issues give rise to debates over theories, methods, principles, and approaches to resolve them.

I feel that our society urgently needs the everyday witness of Christians who take seriously the meaning of the words *ethical, moral, right*, and *wrong*. Our inability to agree on basic problem-solving plans is eroding our confidence, and many of our efforts to tackle the problems we face are failing. Therefore, it seems to me, that the restoration of traditional moral disciplines would be one thing that could direct us toward finding a unified beginning. A moral discipline would, at a minimum, keep us focused on our commitment to address our problems in a manner that would help us to remember what our social and moral responsibilities are. If we are ever going to be hopeful about the possibility of living in peace, justice must prevail and solutions must be created for the good of all the community. "What ever we may think about the social challenges of our age, the fact remains, that in the course of human history," says Kenneth R. Melchin in *An Introduction to Christian Ethics*, "ethics, morals, and social justice, when practiced in light of our Christian faith would produce a society which would understand and accept responsibility for their actions, one that would open their hearts to God with little to be concerned about, and living with other people would promote the dignity of all persons."

Do you think when people make it a habit to accept the responsibility for their actions that it makes it also easier for them to live their live as a better Christian?

| Chapter Two | *Importance Of Ethics, Integrity, And Morality In Building A Code Of Conduct* |

"Is there one rule which a man could live by for his whole life?" asked a student of the master.

"What you do not want done to yourself do not do to others," answered Confucius. "The good man who wishes to provide for himself will provide for others: if he wishes to better himself, he will better others. This is the underlying principal of my teaching." (**1**)

In a collection of Confucius's sayings entitled, *The Analects*, Confucius taught that the most important virtue of an individual was his "character." He taught that character was the major ingredient at the core of an acceptable moral and ethical behavior. He told his students, "The man of honor thinks often of his character, the inferior man of his position. The man of honor desires justice, the inferior man favor." He continues his discussion by talking about ways in which man can improve one's character, "Take conscientiousness and sincerity as your ruling principles, submit also your mind to right conditions, and your character will improve."(**2**) He asks students, "If a man put duty first and success after, will not that improve his character? If he attacks his own failings instead of those of others, will he not remedy his personal faults?" (**3**)

Because character development, in my opinion, is influenced positively or negatively by moral and ethical principles, I feel it is important to know what those principles are and what influence they have on the development of character. Learning how to recognize them and understanding their influence during the developmental process of character is a major first step in improving one's stature among members of society. Understanding the spirit in which things are founded and developed should help us to recognize the influence a moral and ethical character will have on our future. Knowing why things are the way they are, how things work, and why our society acts the way it does will help this process.

Principles That Build Character: At the forefront of character development are the abstract concepts of respect, justice, honesty, compassion, and integrity. These are the major ingredients that help to create a moral and ethical excellence. Their development, however, requires an extensive learning process before they can be part of a mature character. This process involves several critical stages, each of which contributes significantly to the adult developmental process that includes education, life experiences, and time. Stimulating the journey to maturity are testing periods that act to shape and reshape the behavioral concepts developed along life's journey toward a final code of conduct. At this point, standards of integrity have been formed, which work to compliment the developing adult character.

Depending on the level of education desired and the life experiences which have influenced a person's avocations and vocations, the learning process does not usually culminate until all educational goals have been reached, a socially well balanced code of conduct is being maintained, and one is satisfied that his level of character development has been achieved and is projecting an acceptable moral and ethical standard of behavior. Determining one's social acceptance within the community and judging whether one's code of conduct properly compliments one's level of skills, education, and experiences obtained is society.

Whether one has been influenced to pursue academics or scientific endeavors, athletics, sales and marketing, arts, or engineering, it is the personal involvement he has had with life experiences that usually determines his final decision as to what to become and the length of time it takes for its accomplishment. What he has perceived as being his only interest derived from his life experiences may become the only thing he wants to do; maybe it is just different from anyone else's interest that he knows. When desires are achieved, pleasures are received. Bertrand Russell points out, "A man's first duty is to himself and that to secure his own good is more imperative than to secure other peoples." The common belief is considered by Russell to mean, "The ends which one man ought to pursue are different from those which another man ought to pursue." **(4)**

While pleasure is probably the motivation, we have all known what I call the "loner egotist." The name is not intended to mean that I think this type will not become a person of integrity or display a proper moral or ethical behavior according to a rational society, it simply means this type will probably not be very eager to participate in community affairs, will not likely influence, inspire, or share their talent with others, unless those they come in contact have the same interests and goals. His lack of interest in other things does not require him to give any consideration or thought to whether or not his code of conduct would be appropriate for all others to adopt or if his actions would result in a benefit to the common good although it is possible that it could. Instead, they proceed to travel a road, which requires little or no attention be given to any negative responses they may receive from those with different interest, nor do they care what others think. I might add, developing such a code of conduct is fine, provided it supports a morality that emphasizes good instead of evil. This type character can be flawed, however, if the "loner egotist" develops the philosophy "do what I say and not what I do" in an attempt to justify his independent behavior. However, as Russell says, "The mere fact that a man will derive some pleasure from achieving his object is no reason for saying that his desire is self-centered." **(5)**

When comparing the code of conduct of a loner egotist with one who has the same level of intelligence and education but maintains other interests, we find an introvert, good at one thing such as philosophy or medical research. This is the kind who would be likely to discover a cure for cancer someday as opposed to an extrovert who would be more involved with the physical or social concerns of his society. While both may have an acceptable concept of right and wrong, their character will not reflect the same behavior, good or bad, because of their different level of involvement with others. To avoid any possible entrapment toward developing a copycat code of conduct, it is important to accept one's limitations and constantly work hard to reach the highest level of proficiency obtainable in one's chosen profession. Expanding one's horizons, whether by participating in sports for recreational or professional purposes, hobbies, civic activities, or church ministries will help to develop the concepts of respect, justice, compassion, and integrity, which are important in developing a strong character. Additional skills increase one's value to society and increase one's personal confidence. Becoming the best we can become at what we do and simply doing the right thing above all other possibilities is a sign of integrity and character, which provides others the incentive to consider such a person as worth knowing.

Do What's Right and God Will Take Care of You: Stephen Crane in his wonderful novel about the Civil War, *The Red Badge of Courage*, writes about a young Henry Fleming, who, for all the wrong reasons, thinks he can gain a hero's reputation by going to war. Henry recalls, before his first battle, his mother's advice after he tells her about his intentions to enlist in the army. She says, "Henry, I don't want yeh to ever do anything, Henry, that yeh would be 'shamed to let me know about, jest think as if I was a-watchin' yeh. If yeh keep that in yer mind allus, I guess yeh'll come out about right." She concluded her advice by saying, "If so be a time comes when yeh have a to be kilt or do a mean thing, why Henry, don't think of anything 'cept what's right, . . . and the Lord'll take keer of us all." **(6)** People sometimes think they can gain respect for all the wrong reasons by doing what they think people want them to do. Henry desires the prestige that he thinks his education and religion will not give him. When he finally faces battle, however, he becomes another person. The reality he faced changed his desire for fame and winning a name for himself as he says, "It was difficult to think of reputation when others were thinking of skins." **(7)** Henry does finally earn his reputation and learns what it means to be called a man. His character had been changed by his experiences in the war. His romantic and adolescent interpretations of what manhood was and how to gain a reputation had matured substantially because of his experiencing the realities of battle. After capturing the enemy's flag, he knew that he had become a man of courage, and no one had to tell him so. He learned a harsh lesson about life and what disregard for another human life meant, was that right? His mother's advice echoed in his memory, "Henry, don't think of anything 'cept what's right, . . . and the Lord'll take keer of us all." **(8)** Henry had experienced the reality of war and learned some hard lessons of life when he realized that the world goes on whether you're in it or not and that all life meets the same end sooner or later. He must have realized then that those principles that build character are sometimes not easy to learn.

A lot of soldiers got religious when faced with death, others lived and died knowing that all the "good" in the world is represented in Jesus, the proper lifestyle, the divine standard for morality who came to fulfill the law and the prophets (Matt. 5:17-18), and that the heart of the law, which is the ten commandments, is the core of the biblical ethic for all Christians to follow. Jesus taught, as recorded in John 15:12-13, "No one has greater love than this, to lay down one's life for one's friends." And he did exactly that! Christ promised to send the same Spirit that empowered Him to enable us to do His works (John 14:12; 16:7) and to bear fruit of love (Gal. 5:22). Thus, the virtues that bear the fruit of love are the virtues that create the principles that build character: patience, kindness, generosity, faithfulness, gentleness, and self-control. Jesus reminds us not to be conceited, provoke one another, or envious of one another. He says if we live in the Spirit, let us also follow the Spirit (Gal. 5:23-26). The very heart of Christian ethic—the life that demonstrates the principle of the cross in all of Christian conduct and behavior—is emphasized by our Lord when he said, "I always do the things that are pleasing to him" (John 8:29). "I do not seek my own will, but the will of Him who sent Me" (John 5:30). "I have come down from heaven not to do my own will, but the will of Him, who sent me" (John 6:38). **(9)**

Thinking of others first is not a common trait many possess these days. Unfortunately, looking out for number one seems to have taken over top billing in many people's lives and has become the act responsible for making them lose sight of their more Christian responsibilities. This attitude is usually most prevalent in people who work for their own agenda. These are self-driven, power-seeking persons who refuse to recognize what their limitations as a colleague, parent, spouse, or friend have become. Very often, they do not respond to these obligations in favor of impressing those whom they believe to be in a position to advance their self-righteous image. Their thirst for power often produces an absolute separation between themselves and their family in favor of their societal acquaintances who, ironically, are competing for the same influential positions. As the competition increases, their self-indulgent behavior produces temporary gains but long-term catastrophic results. One of the main things people with grand egos do not learn to accept is the fact that multicultural means different ideas, beliefs, and behaviors from their own. This lack of understanding is why turmoil exists. Working hard is not wrong if we are striving to improve the lives of others as well as our own. It takes hard work to compromise, cooperate, and respect different ideas while trying to reach a solution that will produce a better life for all concerned. If we would all choose to face the future with the desire and purpose of creating a life designed with best interest of the common good as our goal, we would find our future exciting again. If everyone would work with the proper balance of faith, trust, respect, and "jest do what's right," they would find good things happening to them as well.

IT WOULD BE NICE if we individually expanded our enthusiasm for attending church every week. It would be nice if we did those things that help make this a kinder world. Finally, it would be nice if we would concentrate on those activities and ministries that work to make the right thing to do a habit. When a person of religious character exercises his political freedom, for example, he or she is more inclined to make those decisions that are in the best interest of the common good. I am convinced, the person who practices an ethical behavior based on strong religious principles will produce a behavioral attitude worthy of praise and will be a creator of great accomplishments. The choices he makes and the way he expresses his thoughts will make him more acceptable to his peers and will gain for him the respect of the fast majority of his associates and those he meets. People with a strong character are more likely to accept the responsibility to try as hard as they can to find an agreeable solution beneficial to all, which is no easy task I agree, but they will try. People with character leave no suggestion of doubt as to their intentions.

We have had many examples of statesmen, philanthropists, church leaders, teachers, etc., throughout the history of our young country that was said to have been a person of strong character. One who stands out in my mind was Dorothy Day, who was a person who "prayed for the gift of faith." **(10)** She was the founder of the *The Catholic Worker*, which was a monthly social conservative newspaper in which she championed for the rights of the poor and used the New Testament as her primary source for its ethical guidance. She was a champion of the common good, and her legacy of inspiration was a challenge to all. She was a person of strong character "because she lived out what she believed; it was not what Dorothy Day wrote that was extraordinary, nor even what she believed, but the fact that there was absolutely no distinction between what she believed, what she wrote, and the manner in which she lived." **(11)** Some will maintain the philosophy "do what I say and not what I do," but not Dorothy. One's character and integrity should never need to be doubted or questioned, and one's behavior should always reflect a sincere concern for avidity for moral thinking and conduct.

While it is true that we do not live in a utopian world, we do live in a Godly world. I think it is possible to be cautious and protective of our family and love ones while being ethical and morally sound when trying to make this a better world to live in today for tomorrow. We have an obligation to teach our legacies as much as we are able and as much as they are capable of learning, but most importantly, it is our obligation to lead the way by example. For those individuals who have sufficient intelligence to process the knowledge required to understand the kinds of acts that morality prohibits, requires, and endorses, a character for all to emulate and trust will result. As Dr. Laura Schlessinger writes, "Values inform our conscience which influences our behavior. Our behavior determines the quality of our lives and the meaningfulness of our personal contributions to others, to life, and to history." **(12)**

GOD'S MORAL RULES ARE THE BUILDING BLOCKS OF AN ETHICAL CHARACTER: Ever since the early days of Genesis, many societies have existed. All of them had great intentions and admirable objectives while a few even enjoyed some degree of success. The main ingredients they seemed to have forgotten in their attempt to create the perfect society was the importance of the part character, morality, and ethics played in the building of a sound community. Things are the way they are today because of this lapse in knowledge. For example, after sending Moses to free His people, God told Moses to give them a covenant that would give them standards to live by. By fulfilling God's commandments, they would be given the opportunity to live a fruitful life. They not only chose to live life using their own rules and disrespecting God, but they also ignored the lessons of history and chose to adopt a moral code of conduct different from that which God had commanded. They were not successful. After the floods eliminated all but Noah and his cargo, God gave them a second chance. Since the goal of any society should be to provide for the mutual concerns of their groups welfare, one of the biggest task society faced was appointing someone to accept the responsibility to be in charge of delegating the authority to perform various roles. While these positions created social importance for those chosen, most leaders forgot that they had the responsibility to expect their citizens to live with a knowledge of God's will based on knowing the difference between right from wrong. The irony was the social prestige of their position made them overlook their obligation to create a moral society, which emphasized good over evil.

ORGANIZING A SOCIETY: It was not until the fifteenth century that the English word *society* appeared with its meaning being closely related to that, which is social, and its major role involved the process of organizing a network of relationships between its group's leaders. Their most demanding task was to develop solutions to the many concerns expressed by the group. It soon became obvious to them that a moral society worked for the common good, but the question that always seemed to arise in every society was, what moral obligation to preserve the common good do we have? In his chapter on the *Ethics of Existentialism*, William Banner says, "The moral life is a continuing resolution of individual crisis, inasmuch as the individual must in every situation decide what he shall do, whatever the alternatives before him, and the reasons for and against each alternative. Moral existence, in other words, is a life of decision and action as well as a debate on moral questions." **(13)**

This was an important question because we live for and await the coming of a community composed of justice and righteousness in which some are last who will be first, and some are first who will be last (Luke 13:30). Many societies who completely and voluntarily abandoned the Christian religion—whether they did it to become worshippers of paganism, Judaism, Mohammedanism, or became a naturalist, rationalists, etc.—spoke to the times and experiences of the people making the decision. Jean-Paul Sartre says, "Man is nothing else but what he makes of himself . . . . But what do we mean by this, if not that man has a greater dignity that a stone or tablet? For we mean that man first exists, that is, that a man first of all is the being who hurls himself towards a future and who is conscious of imagining himself as being in the future." **(14)**

Becoming an apostate is to deny the religion itself, which, in the eyes of God, is a sin of the most grievous type. There were many failed societies that lacked the belief in God; but as we learned in the New Testament, the community Jesus wants to establish will always be under his protection. Only the power of Jesus can be called upon to protect us from all dangers, "O you of Little Faith" (Matt. 8:26). The repetitive theme in His teachings, which assures us of His protection, is threefold: (1) Be prepared for the second coming, (2) treat one another with love and respect, and (3) kept the faith and remember that the risen Christ is present and powerful to those who have faith.

The fundamental principle for the existence of a moral society is the result that it achieves when it requires all its members to work together and its code of conduct to maintain a lessening of evil or harm as its goal. The process of working together requires an attitude of active participation and cooperation, and since the result that is achieved by authorities and citizens is common to all, this is called the common good. Therefore, it is important that the results achieved in the development of this end be protected. The rights and duties of those involved in developing the social conditions, which will be conducive to a moral and spiritual life needs laws, man-made and spiritual, so that a positive effect on the common good can reflect a spirit of unification, pride, and moral soundness. Legislation, which creates man-made laws, must be made with the common good in mind; however, legislation cannot create a moral people. The duties of achieving the common good task, however, rest primarily with two groups: (1) the public sector and (2) the private sector. The public sector is responsible for making the laws, overseeing justice, and providing protection for the community; and the private sector has to do with family matters. It is important for both sectors to maintain the common good objective because it is necessary that they work together while promoting the production and distribution of goods, the promotion of scientific research, protection for its people, and maintaining a respect for the arts. We ask, "Who gets to decide when social changes are necessary and how they should be changed? Is this the role of protestors, the lobbyist, those with other agendas, or the persons of good character, moral, and ethical principles?" You make the call!

The reason we act the way we do is because our society is very much influenced by how it perceives intellect and regards morality. John Dewey once said, "We only think when confronted with a problem," to which I have two questions:

1. How may one communicate using sources of knowledge, which are not available through ordinary thought?

2. How do known sources of knowledge, available only to the highly educated, become available to those seeking answers?

Should we not distinguish between reason and intellect here?—the earlier having to do with the production of ideas, which can be accomplished by most thinkers, the latter with their realization, which takes intellect. Are we sometimes prone to confuse thinking with "intelligence and act" because they have to do with the completion of ideas, which are the product of imaginative thinking and not so much the degree of superior intellect? Dewey suggests that intelligence consists of

- a set of flexible and growing habits that involve sensitivity,
- imagination that is exercised in seeing new possibilities and hypotheses,
- willingness to learn from experience,
- fairness and objectivity in judging and evaluating conflicting values and opinions, and
- the courage to change one's views when it is demanded by the consequences of our actions.

He continues by saying, "An intelligent person is sensitive to the practical demands of situations and knows how far to carry his deliberations. In those situations in which immediate action is demanded, the funded experience of the intelligent person guides his action." **(15)** For example, imaginative thinking, when used in comparing art with the scriptures, requires that one examine the purpose of the work. Art, in my opinion, is a personal presentation of a particular subject, which is expressed by an artist for his own purposes. The art form itself represents the artist's view of what the subject means, looks like, or represents to him. He usually paints for pleasure and relies on his ability to produce the desired results. The art form's meaning depends on the position the artist has taken in selecting the methods he will use to present his subject and the form he has selected in his presentation of the subject. In Dewey's *Art as Experience*, he says, "Art has a moral function in civilization, but not be being moralistic or didactic. The moral function of art is exercised by the imaginative projection and presentation of ideals." **(16)**

The sacred scriptures, on the other hand, are God's inspired words written by a human author. The writer usually is addressing a particular group (the faithful) in hopes they will better understand the will of God. Both require results, which either accepts or rejects the work. One would therefore interpret an art form much as one interprets the scriptures. Both artist and writer work with a passion, are not often understood, and reflect a love in their work, which is reflected in their final product produced. In order to understand the work of either talent, one must be knowledgeable and possess a lived or knowledgeable relationship between the interpreter and the object. Therein lays the problem. Art requires imagination and scripture requires faith. Most who are highly intelligent because of their educational experience have trouble generating significant thoughts based on a creative or religious faith based experience.

If good and evil was a result of Adam and Eve's choices and how in man's future knowledge would be used, then it could be said that history became a by-product of man's choices. Because of choices, history measures the worthiness of man's decisions and what he has done with the power to act. The sin of evil became the sin of disobedience to God, and death was the result; did man make a bad decision? Theologian Bernard Lonergan says, when people respond to the problems of caring for others—such as to prevent social tragedies, to protect weaker members from exploitation, and to coordinate people into common action to accomplish, and sustain what none could achieve on their own—moral rules arise. Moreover, says Lonergan, people seek to promote and instill moral rules out of a sense of personal responsibility. When this happens, a sense of moral "socialization" harnesses this responsibility, which then becomes operative in us and directs these responsibilities toward the objectives devised and chosen by others who were mobilized by a similar experience. If we agree that society is organized for the good of its members, both individually and collectively, then the dignity of the human person requires the pursuit of the common good and the spirit of cooperation must prevail. **(17)**

CONTRIBUTING TO THE COMMON GOOD REQUIRES AN AWARENESS OF NEEDS: Over the years, I have observed that most people are not "totally aware" of who or what they are, what role they are playing in life, how to act, or how to treat people when exposed to an uncomfortable environment much less think about what's good for others. By awareness, I don't mean that they do not know when to say, "Thank you," "Yes, sir," or "Let me help you with that," I mean they do not take the time or have the capacity to smell fresh coffee brewing, hear the birds sing, or to see the love which made the flowers grow in a natural way and not the way one was taught or told how things should be. It is important to learn and understand the games people play and the situations that people put us in before we can gain the luxury of experiencing freedom from boredom, stress from painful experiences, and what to do when they raise their nasty heads. The joy of participating in life's opportunities only comes when we maintain an open mind and become aware of our community, its requirements, and the people whom we are associated with from a different perspective. In Gaudium et Spes, the Church in the Modern World, the *common good* is defined as "the sum total of social conditions which allow people, either as groups or as individuals to reach their fulfillment more fully and more easily." **(18)**

In his analysis, Marvin L. Hair Mich, writes, Gaudium et Spes "presents the church's understanding of the dignity of the human person—endowed with freedom, intelligence, and moral sensitivity. Human dignity and human nature are essentially social." He then quotes paragraph 12, "By their innermost nature persons are social beings and unless they relate themselves to others they can neither live nor develop their potential."**(19)** The common good contains three essential elements, each of which imposes serious responsibilities on the community including: (1) respect of the person, (2) social well-being and development, and (3) peace. These human rights, given our supernatural destiny and relationship with God, are not just economic, social, or political rights but must center around essential spiritual and moral rights—the ability to act according to conscience and freedom of religion. To be "totally aware," one needs to understand how to acquire and share those necessities, skills, and virtues, which are required in order to live a genuine human life and contribute to the common good. These include providing food, clothing, housing, and other essentials required to maintain a standard of living conducive to the raising and protection of families, providing for education, work, and maintaining a good name. A behavior, which shows respect for others, acquires knowledge, acts to the dictates of a moral conscience, and safeguards individual privacy, rightful freedom, and includes participation in matters of a personal religion is a behavior which will successfully bear fruit.

Developing a lifestyle with these characteristics does not require a PhD from Harvard. What it does require is a common sense implementation of principles learned from our religious and secondary education, tradition, and experience. As it is written in Pacem in Terris, "Man's social order requires constant improvement; it must be founded in truth, built on justice and enlivened by love. It should grow in freedom towards a more humane equilibrium before man can become very aware of his value and the contributions he can make to the betterment of the society in which he lives." (**20**) Philosophies are created after a society has demonstrated an acceptable universal morality, which has been developed because of a responsible and accepted ethic. Within the framework of that philosophy lays the very influences that causes the philosophy to mature and from the characteristics of the people within that society comes their culture. What one group finds acceptable is based on the criteria and materials they had to work with but often creates a different culture in another group. Because of the need for an authority to see that the conditions of a proper life are maintained, the developed philosophy finds itself influenced by various types of societies because of the freedom brought about by the choices and values of its members.

IF TALENT, INTEGRITY, AND ETHICS INFLUENCES OUR EVALUATION OF CRAFTSMEN, WHY DOESN'T IT INFLUENCE OUR EVALUATION OF OTHERS? We have all been required to make judgments that have had an important effect on our future. The friends and business relationships we have generated is a direct result of and reflection on our character; but then, what is it in strangers, such as doctors, airline pilots, and chefs that beget a legitimate expectation that they will not betray our trust? It is very easy to grant professionals a stamp of approval and assume they possess a moral ethic and integrity. Why is that? In my opinion, this is because they are required to earn and always maintain an acceptable degree of competence in their chosen field. They have been required to complete years of formal education, participate in supervised and stringent on-the-job training, and successfully complete proficiency tests before they may offer their services to the public.

Whether or not they are persons of character depends on their behavior and not their profession, but we automatically trust them to perform their skills professionally with a great degree of confidence because of the reasons already given. Most artisans, on the other hand, are not required to have as much formal academic education but are bound to a code of ethics governing the performance of the job skill they are performing and are required to complete continuing education requirements annually in order to keep their license to operate. Their training comes from several years of technical schools and many years of on-the-job supervised training. They must maintain acceptable industry standards, be subjected to the rules of a professional licensing body, and may be disciplined for not maintaining ethical and professional standards. A worker's reputation determines his longevity in his chosen profession and is usually an indication of the public's acceptance of his competence—his badge of approval if you will.

It is these professional standards and requirements that we are trusting and not the person's character. Whether he or she maintains any degree of longevity will be determined by the quality of service they provide. Their business integrity and moral behavior will be reflected by the standards they practice and the growth they experience in the community. Whether they are a person of good moral and ethical character will be determined by the results of their job performance, reputation, and social behavior. On the other hand, there are people we have known a lifetime to be of good character but in whom we are still reluctant to place our trust. Of course, it depends on what sort of trust in their actions we need. For example, a fellow I have known for a long time who has worked at a gas station all his life would not be the one I would trust to fix my computer, but he may be a very trust worthy friend to tell a secret.

Trust and faith in persons who become our friend usually are earned because of the character they reflect and not by their degree of formal education, number of skills acquired, or social status attained. On the other hand, the trust and faith we might have in a person's ability to perform a particular skill is dependent on what type of experience and formal training they have had and not their character. The longevity and successes achieved in performing that skill successfully over a long period, however, is dependent on the person's character and integrity. Thus, it is a combination of a person's social behavior, morality, integrity, and degree of training that make up the core virtues that determine character, trust, and the confidence others feel.

TRUST IS AN IMPORTANT VIRTUE TO HAVE: There are those I have known a lifetime who have been blessed with skills and talent but project a suspicious personality. Usually, this analysis is based on what is considered to be a lack of acceptable social and business finesse on the part of the craftsman. Because of their overpowering, know-it-all attitude, it is difficult to accept the possibility that they might have some concern for one's problem but easy to accept that they indeed have a great interest in one's wallet. It is difficult to trust that such a person will perform services in your best interest. We have all heard stories of tricks pulled on owners of RVs and automobile fraud artists on tourists who were far from home. It is hard to imagine the money that was given up to these unscrupulous crooks. Then there are those who seem to project their interest in your job by the amount of services you require because of the revenue it will produce.

It is true, skill and knowledge is what successfully completes the job and not the craftsman's personality, even though it reflects the probability that he will not win any Sunday school awards for compassion. Faith and trust in the person or company providing services is important, but ultimately, it is the artisan's ethics or the company's reputation for being a quality firm that develops the faith and trust that creates their long-term success. Therefore, it seems to me, that trust is gained when an artisan becomes proficient in the skills required to accomplish the tasks required and is able to reflect confidence and pride in his workmanship to the customer. Sometimes, artisans earn the reputation for overcharging for their talent and develop a "you get what you pay for" attitude; but if the quality of their work is consistently competent, their concept of a fair and reasonable price is soon accepted by the public and their longevity becomes assured. Reputations, good or bad, are earned by performance; but character is earned by social behavior. The question is, would you rather have a skilled and highly qualified electrician with a lousy personality repairing your wiring problem or a young man full of charm who just completed his final test in electrical wiring from a long distance correspondence school?

BECOME THE BEST YOU CAN BE: It seems to me, therefore, that it should always be one's goal, regardless of academic ability, to become as skilled at one's job as possible, to act with compassion for those that asks us for help, and reflect a trustworthy ethic. We should think, communicate, and act in the best interest of the common good, and live by the principles of a theology that promotes respect for human dignity. We should strive to support those solutions, which reflect the best results for the person who has placed his trust in us; and always maintain an attitude that wants to become the person respected and called reliable by friends, customers, associates, and those we meet in pursuit of our day-to-day activities.

This type of attitude, built on trust, would make this world a much better place to live. Trust and faith is necessary when decisions are made, and we trust that they will be made in the best interest of the community's needs. We have faith that the role of those who are formulating the procedures to follow in making those decisions are morally motivated to make fair and balanced solutions. Solutions resulting from a cooperative attitude lead to solutions, which bring about a just and tolerant result for a common cause and usually reflect a degree of compromise on everyone's part. A fair and just balance of many attitudes usually prevails when we are trying to bring about a balanced, just, and tolerant result for a common cause. The process of thinking about how to utilize and present fair and just possibilities when making decisions affecting most people will usually produce a more suitable solution for the community as well as one's self. With this in mind, we can understand why it is important to show how necessary it is to develop a character, which reflects a respect for a morality, which represents a socially acceptable behavior, values human dignity, and respects cultural differences.

GOD's PLAN FOR US IS NOT ALWAYS KNOWN: As we continue to develop new ways to challenge our thinking and create ways to accomplish our goals, it just might be possible, somewhere along the way, to change a negative attitude into a positive one. I believe, however, we should become more socially conscious of our need to be charitable before we can find better solutions. Only when we are able to understand and explain to others what human rights are and what respect for human life means will we be able to promote peace and love for our neighbor. It is more helpful to listen with the intent of being helpful than critical. You may have experienced, sometime in your life, that wonderful feeling you get when you realize that someone is truly concerned about your problem and is making an honest effort to find a solution. This is the feeling that causes attitudes to change and biased opinions to be compromised.

God's plan for us is not often known; and although there is good in the things man does in the world, fame, fortune, and happiness does not always prevail. Life is an ambiguous state of being which is beyond man's capacity to understand. To be perfect, for example, required that Adam and Eve not eat from the tree of knowledge, but because they did, what resulted was an inheritance for all of us consisting of hard work, challenges, and the ability to make choices. Because of knowledge, we learned that evil exists in our world; the degree to which we experience it is dependent on the choices we make. The book of Ecclesiastes, the Bible chapter mostly concerned with the purpose and value of life, reminds us that it is "God" who has made everything appropriate to its time and has put the timelessness into their hearts without man's ever discovering, from beginning to end, the work which God has done (Eccles. 3:11-15). Qoheleth, a teacher of popular wisdom and the literary name of the author of Ecclesiastes said to be David's son, king in Jerusalem, "I recognized that there is nothing better than to be glad and to do well during life. For every man, moreover, to eat, drink, and enjoy the fruit of all his labor is a gift from God. I recognized that whatever God does will endure forever, there is no adding to it, or taking from it. Thus has God done that he may be revered. What now is as already been, what is to be, already is; and God restores what would otherwise be displaced." Thanks to God should be given for all the pleasures we have been blessed to posses; it will be God who is the final judge of what is good and bad. Qoheleth's epilogue concludes his advice, "The last word, when all is heard: Fear God and keep his commandments, for this is man's all; Because God will bring to judgment every work, with all its hidden qualities, whether good or bad" (Eccles.12:13-14).

STUDENTS ARE LEARNING HOW TO PREPARE: In today's business climate, for example, employers are looking to see whether or not their current and potential employees can exhibit a moral and ethical response when required to make business decisions involving important and sometimes controversial issues. HR supervisors are remiss if they do not know how their employees will act in crucial situations. They must be satisfied that the employee will follow the company's established code of conduct when faced with situations requiring an ethical response. In this "sue for all reasons" culture, an attempt to keep the company's exposure to law suites at a minimum, while producing a bottom line that keeps the business financially healthy, is extremely necessary. In today's business classes, students are given a set of circumstances that could cause a potentially threatening liability and are trained to ask certain questions that will help them make the right decisions. By teaching them how to analyze the facts, make proper assumptions, and draw conclusions that are just, fair, ethical, and in the best interest of all concerned, the situation is resolved.

DOING WHAT IS RIGHT REQUIRES THOUGHT, COMPROMISE, AND RESPECT: What is right or wrong can depend on a majority opinion and not on the conclusion that would be reached by any one individual. This could lead to an attitude of going with the flow or agreeing with the most influential member of the staff. Complicating the matter even more can be cultural values. To an American family, a steak dinner, for example, is something special to be enjoyed when going out to celebrate a special occasion; but if your guest is a family from India, the cow is taboo and would not be appropriate. Since every action has the potential of influencing someone in a negative manner, we must give thought to each of our proposed solutions in light of the attitude the resulting environment may produce. If we applied the greatest good principle, it would be a matter of how many would be offended and how many would enjoy the meal, but then, we could run into the situation that there may be those who are vegetarian and could care less if you served meat or not but would be offended if you didn't have vegetables for them to eat. We are now faced with another concept of character called respect and compassion. So far, we have seen that morality relates to behavior, that ethics involves honesty, and that justice is treating people fairly, and now there is respect and compassion to be considered. People who feel sympathetic to the problems of others display compassion. So we ate pizza, half with pepperoni and half vegetarian.

LEND A HELPING HAND WHEN YOU CAN: Maybe you have seen people with the same cultural background behave in a manner different from that, which is considered to be our learned or customary behavior. I have also noted that some people who are from foreign countries seem to live by a code of conduct similar to their native beliefs and customs regardless of whether or not these actions are acceptable behavior to their native neighbors. I am particularly discouraged when I see people taking advantage of all this country has to offer, for a long period, but cannot or will not learn our language. Maybe these people are unaware of what their acceptable actions should be when confronted with various social situations because they do not understand how to ask for an explanation of what to do.

In the past, I have assumed that either their lack of ability to know what to do was caused by a lack of education or their experience was limited. However, today, given the fact that they all have the same opportunities to learn, I have to conclude that they probably do not know how to act because they have not availed themselves of the opportunities to learn the language, the customs, or what the proper behavior should be. However, I get the impression that they seem to expect me to understand their customs, language, and lifestyle without flaw.

Motivation and incentives to do the right things should be learned at home, but all too often, there is no one who cares or there is no one capable of providing the proper guidance. A positive environment, if available, can be all a person needs to inspire him to do better. If we know that there is no one that is going to be a positive influence, especially to young people, this is the perfect time to become involved with those who will appreciate the help in learning the difference between good and bad. If there is no foundation for knowing or experiencing the difference between what is good and bad, what is acceptable or unacceptable, the choice that is easier to make or the choice that will give the most immediate result is the road most often traveled. What seems to be the easy way out, however, can lead to crime, jail, or even death. How many generations can experience these conditions and survive to make a difference or become a positive influence to the next generation? To recognize that someone needs a little help with their life or someone to become a big brother, big sister, mentor, friend, or an influential guidance counselor is what Jesus inferred when he said, "What you do for my brother you do for me." How many dreams have come true when someone who could provide them with an opportunity to improve recognized young adults with talent?

PRACTICE THE GOLDEN RULE: If "do unto others as you would have them do unto you" is the glue that binds a society together, then a morality that discourages doing harm or prohibits one from being evil should produce a society of rational people. However, since we are the product of one's genetics and behavioral philosophy, a distorted image of what one's "code of conduct" can become is often the result of evil overriding the characteristics of what moral behavior should produce. Motivating us to become immoral criminals includes greed, self-interest, personal pleasures, a lack of compassion, and fear, to name a few. John Steinbeck in his award-winning novel, *East of Eden*, created a character that portrayed the exact opposite of what any Christian ethical person would be in Joe Valery. Joe had his own "code of conduct," which was far from acceptable to most members of his society but would certainly be understood and acceptable by street gang members, pimps, and other types of criminals looking to steal whatever was available for their own purpose. "'Hate cannot live alone,' Joe Valery said. 'It must have love as a trigger, a goad, or a stimulant.'" **(21)**

Accompanying Joe's way of life was Cathy, or if she was trying to disguise her identity, she was called Kate, who was created by Steinbeck to represent the epitome of an evil mind. Joe works for Cathy's brothel as a bouncer. Cathy or Kate, when she was a young girl, murdered her parents and then became a prostitute. Later, she shot her husband, abandoned her sons, and committed an additional murder in order to gain control of the brothel. To assure her longevity in her chosen profession, she took pictures of the town's most prominent customers doing very lewd acts with her girls so that she could use them for blackmail if necessary. She used drugs to control and manipulate her whores. Cathy is used by Steinbeck to represent evil in the world similar to how the writer in Genesis used Eve after he introduces the readers to sin. In the end, Cathy commits suicide after learning that her son had killed himself when he was told that she was his mother. The innocent suffers for the sins of others seems to be the point. Prior to her committing suicide, her health was becoming worse. As it was disintegrating, Joe took over more control of her brothel. In a final blow of evil versus evil, Cathy informs the police about Joe's escape from jail just in case he tries to leave town with her money. After she is dead, the police gun him down as he tries to escape. Joe's code of conduct is no different from Cathy's; she is just more evil. She knew how to create power and held it over her girls and Joe. Joe developed an admiration for her as well, based on fear. The girls knew that if they followed the rules she laid down and followed them exactly, Cathy would take care of them and protect them. There was no love involved and no respect. She never rewarded them, and she punished an offender only twice before she removed her. The girls did have the security of knowing that they would not be punished without cause. Joe's set of rules might have gone like this:

> Don't believe nobody, the bastards are after you. Keep your mouth shut. Don't stick your neck out. Keep your ears open. When they make a slip, grab on to it and wait. Everybody is a son of a bitch and whatever you do, they got it coming. Go at everything roundabout. Don't never trust no dame about nothing. Put your faith in dough. Everybody wants it everybody will sell out for it. **(22)**

Sometimes, one's ethical conduct is foreshadowed by the behavior reflected in past situations. Since the cause to act is based on one's morality, which is at the core of one's character, it can be concluded that morality is the major ingredient in molding one's behavior. Ethics and morality combine to create the type of character that will make up one's personality. For example, Eve was persuaded by an overwhelming desire for the promised knowledge she could gain from eating the apple from the forbidden tree of knowledge, according to the devil-snake, that she was willing to disobey our Lord's rule of not eating from the tree of knowledge. Although eating is not evil in itself, she sacrificed her favor with God for the possibility of achieving something she did not have, **knowledge**. She became someone who could not be trusted to do the right thing (not eat the apple) because her desire for power overruled her faith in God. The temptation to gain (self-interest) knowledge, to make her something she was not, was her motivation. Her ethics asked, "How do I do this if I decide to do it?" But if it's wrong, her morality was saying, "I can blame someone else if it doesn't work out." Since her character lacked the ability to recognize what the consequences of her actions would be (her act to disobey God's "will") what she did created "sin." Thus, the Genesis author used the Adam and Eve story for several purposes: How did I get here, how can we be responsible for our choices without knowledge or experience, and why do the innocent suffer? Faith and trust had escaped her character.

FAITH AND TRADITIONS MOTIVATE ACTIONS: If the mind at birth has no meaningful intelligence and is developed and shaped by its desires, then it makes sense that a society who wants, for example, the strongest army only need to control the experience of those capable of learning military techniques. When they have developed the proper physical maturity and age to become proficient, they go into action. If there are two purposes for education, (1) to teach people how to do things and (2) preparing people to live a life, why isn't our moral behavior controlled by our education and behavior? To know what is acceptable and not acceptable would become dependent on the rules made by our leaders.

The problem is, not everyone is going to play by the same rules. Because of this probability, education, religion, reason, politics, and class structure play a very important part in our success to make rational solutions. History has developed a procedure for us to follow, i.e., how things should have been done based on how it was done, and education or learned experiences make it easier to avoid the mistakes of the past. Passed experiences are valuable contributors to our ability to reason what kind of outcome should result from a given set of specific circumstances. Faith, combined with tradition, becomes a strong influence on those who respect and care about their religious future and makes them better prepared to deal with the consequences of their behavior. The faithful depend on the promises of God and look forward with love to participate in the role they will play in making life better for all. Faith will also play a huge role in the decision-making process in their future. What we learn formally and what we learn from experience and tradition, combined with the faith of our religious philosophy, will contribute greatly to our ability to make reasonable decisions, which in turn is what motivates our moral conduct.

Sometimes the wrong emotions and desires creep into our better judgment, causing our other wise, acceptable, moral behavior to be compromised. Obeying the law is another choice we must make but can sometimes present for us ethical conflicts that do not rest on whether or not crime pays but rather a "what's in for me attitude" or "it's just not fair" justifications. Sometimes, the code of conduct acceptable to society conflicts with the code of behavior of other individuals, groups, and even religions. For example, the subjects of immigration and abortion come to mind. In addition, a point of major discussion these days includes positions regarding same-sex marriages and homosexual clergy. The right to life versus pro-choice, compassion for the poor even if they are illegal, the love for God even if they have a same-sex life partner are just some of the more discerning subjects that are causing conflicts among various groups, individuals, and church members. Civil laws have pretty much taken care of the right to life and immigration issues; however, there are many in our society, including religious groups, who do not agree with the law and will work tirelessly to change it. Churches have addressed the gay clergy situation but there remain those with differences of opinions as to the issue of respect, one for the other. Civil law has also addressed the issue of same-sex marriages, but even though they are not recognized in forty-six states (as of this writing), there are those who are working very diligently to have such a union recognized in other states. Since acceptance by a culture within a society must be representative of the moral code of the majority of its members or the interpretation of its legal authority, these conflicts will probably be settled in time and by money spent for lobbyist.

As it stands now, individuals in our society are making bad decisions. There seems to be a migration away from Christian ethics in favor of an attitude that values "whatever is best for me." A common attitude seems to portray a lack of interest in solving conflicts, which are not essential to one's personal well-being, physical, emotional, mental, or social betterment; therefore, whatever alternative choice is made will be agreeable if it advances our cause. This attitude is a reflection of what various groups see as their statement of values and reflects that which is only important to their best interest. Today's morality seems to have forgotten to include

- the commandments of God,
- a respect for life,
- justice and reason in developing those practices that minimize harm that people may suffer or the evil they may experience, and a
- discipline based on prescribed natural behavior.

People think moral positions should result in a guide, a type of unified statement to be put forward by society for the good of its people. The problem is, the larger the society, the greater the chance that the same code of conduct, which has been laid out for the benefit of that society, eventually will not be accepted by all its members. Crime, for example, tends to grow when economic conditions causes a reduction in opportunities for its citizens to provide adequate amounts of quality food, clothing, education, shelter, and the jobs to fund such essentials for themselves and their families. When things are not going right, unrest and frustration occurs, which causes its members to shift their positions and loyalties. They find other friends who they think can help them, change groups who support their thinking and causes, replace their church for one who tells them what they want to hear, and in the most extreme case, they even change countries until they find the way of life that supports their standards or can provide them better services. We can conclude from this behavior that morality has no limits to its contents but is to be controlled by the law of the land's majority and its economic conditions. They believe in the moral position, which is the easiest to follow and gives them the most pleasures. They want a unified statement to guide them, tell them what to do, and how to do it. An instruction sheet, if you will, like the code of conduct God gave to Moses to give to his people!

According to Webster, a person's character identifies the pattern of behavior or personality found in an individual. A person's character makes a statement about the quality of one's moral strength, reputation, and self-discipline whereas ethics deal with a person's standards of conduct based on their moral judgment. Ethics are systems of behavior, which may be different from individuals, religions, groups, and professions. Moral principles, while closely related to the standards of ethics, deals with the degree of right or wrong in any particular conduct. The consequences of good and evil live with the faithful forever, and depending on one's degree of love for the teachings of their particular religious philosophy, these consequences usually play a huge role in the results of the decisions they make in life. What we learn, experience, and believe about our religious experiences will contribute greatly to our reasoning, which is what motivates our moral actions. It is the emotions and desires that creep into our better judgment that causes our otherwise acceptable moral behavior to be compromised. Laws and the punishment assigned to breaking them are determined by the choices we make whether they are man's or God's.

RELIGION UNITES BELIEVERS: Our entire Christian religion is based on trust, trust that God through Jesus, defeated death to give us eternal life. However, when our beliefs differ from someone else's, we create an ethical problem. We should therefore recognize the differences that exist among the members of our society, apply common sense actions like respect for others, practice politeness that contributes to harmony, and respect the human need for meaning and value in everyone's life.

When one examines the ethical origins of the major religions, the similarities demand a loyalty to a higher authority to accept the Indian religious ethic, which promotes a reincarnation to another life form. An immoral behavior will result in a bad rebirth; therefore, the objective is to do good in order to enjoy a rebirth into a better life. The whole of our Christian's moral origin is derived from the Ten Commandments God handed down to Moses, particularly the commandment to love God with all our heart, mind, strength, and soul, and to love one's neighbor as oneself and the Golden Rule.

The Jewish ethic has its origin in the Old Testament Torah and deals with moral questions created by the Old Testament law contained in the first five books of the Bible know has the Pentateuch. The Jewish people do not believe in the Father, Son, and Holy Spirit as one and are still waiting for the return of Jesus. Islamic ethics is based on the teachings of the Koran in which believers believe in the word of Allah (God) as given to Muhammad. The Koran says God is all-powerful, compassionate, and that people are responsible for their own actions. It teaches that God's will provide a guide to life, and ethically, it emphasizes honesty, generosity, and social justice. All Muslims must perform five basic duties known as the five pillars of Islam which are (1) make a declaration of faith, (2) pray five times daily, (3) give charity to the poor, (4) fast during Ramadan, and (5) make a pilgrimage to Mecca.

All religions promote respect for human life, do not advocate stealing, refrain from sexual misconduct, do not promote gossip or spread false rumors, and do not believe in overdrinking or taking drugs that are harmful. Some have special indulgences during holy days such as in the Christian observance of Lent. They all seem to say, let your personal experience play a role in your faith and bring it to the table. Your experiences create images, which in turn brings insight, awareness, and finally action. When we operate exclusively from a standpoint of certitude, we are unable to test a new experience against the view of life that we hold. What happens is our current interpretations become absolute, unchanging, and true. It is important to remember Jesus forgave our sins and ultimately gave us the opportunity to respond to new possibilities. The author of the book of Hebrews writes the Bible's most comprehensive description of faith when he says, "Faith is the realization of what is hoped for and evidence of things not seen" (Heb. 11:1-2).

The study of God becomes your process which blossoms into your beliefs—the product. Why does God let man forsake him? God created a challenge to us through the prophets. He used them to vent his dissatisfaction. The prophet's greatest concern is much like that of God, "What is man's future going to be?" Why is man so rebellious when he knows that God is so saddened when man forsakes him? If we believe that nothing can stop God from offering salvation to every human being, why do we need to make excuses for not doing his will? Do what is right, and God will take care of us.

THE TEN COMMANDMENTS ARE THE ORIGIN OF A STRONG CHARACTER: Maybe we need to teach a course in school called The Anatomy of a Code of Conduct that emphasizes the building blocks of what a code of conduct is, how it is developed, what supports its success, longevity, its origin, and how to make it improve as we grow. The course should address questions such as:

1. How is an acceptable Code of Conduct developed?
2. What supports a Code of Conduct's success, longevity, and its origin?
3. What part does morality play in its maturity?
4. What influence does integrity have on character development?
5. What values are represented in individuals who are considered to be persons of strong character?

It should be pointed out in the course that the building of an acceptable code of conduct begins with genetics, but the learning process one experiences controls, changes, and matures it by working to establish a strong character as its by-product. A code of conduct that requires a course of action that demands the right thing be done possesses an ethic, which is desired by a rational society and considered proper and displays an attitude and respect for the cultural attributes of those that make up their society. Our religious faith and values derived from the learning process contributes greatly to a code of conduct as Dr. Laura writes, "We gain character from our decision to obey the Ten Commandments in spite of our limited capability to understand. In life," she says, "a higher idealism and a more profound, just, and consistent morality is only found through the commandments." **(23)**

A code of conduct is a collected group of principles, which creates the standards for our ability to know what is right and wrong. A code of conduct is the behavior we reflect that displays our sense of justice, compassion, respect, and honest social, political, and religious values. A code of conduct is the result of our ethics, integrity, and morality. A code of conduct sets on the foundation of the following:

Ethics is a collected set of principles, creating the standards for right and wrong conduct. The principles of an ethical society promote justice, compassion, respectful and honest social, political, and religious values for its citizens as their behavior.

The origin of ethics is found in the teachings of the Golden Rule from the New Testament. An ethical person promotes justice, displays compassion for others, is honest in his dealing with others, and shows respect for all of God's creation.

Integrity is that behavior or conduct that reflects a moral behavior acceptable by a society that promotes education, experience, intelligence, and tradition as its methods for learning what these principles should become. Its emphasis is on creating a behavior acceptable by a rational society as being in favor of the common good.

Its origin is the Ten Commandments given by God to Moses. A person of integrity is honest, works for the best interest of the common good, promotes justice for all, and repects other cultures and ideas different from his.

Morality is created by the ethics and integrity developed from one's concept of what's right and wrong when viewed as being socially, politically, and religously sound by society. A morality is acceptable when society endorses one's behavior as pocessing those principles, which make his code of conduct good. Its origin comes from the teachings of Jesus.

Its origin comes from the teachings of Jesus as revealed in the holy gospels.

In summary, it is ethics that creates the standards for proper conduct and builds the integrity responsible for our Code of Conduct. The result is a morality, which is a combination of the ethics and integrity acquired which inspires the development of our character.

Laws, conscience, values, and religion are the pillars of behavior, which supplements one's moral behavior and supports one's character. It matures as we grow in education, experience, intelligence, faith, and tradition and are the pillars that create an understanding of what actions derived from our morality are acceptable.

In order for our nation to maintain its title of the United States of America blessed by God, we should not become like the society of Moses who forgot.

MORALITY, ETHICS, INTEGRITY
ARE SUPPORTED BY THE PILLARS OF

VALUES	LAWS	CONSCIENCE	RELIGION

WHICH GROW FROM EDUCATION, EXPERIENCE, INTELLIGENCE, AND TRADITION.

In summary, our code of conduct that we practice from day to day should reflect the standards we have adopted from life's learning experiences. What should result is an integrity that has grown from our respect for the education we received in the classroom, from family tradition, our relationship with other cultures, and everyday life experiences. It is the combination of our developed ethic and integrity that promotes justice, compassion, respectful and honest social, political, and religious values that creates a morality that builds a character dedicated to the success of the common good.

THINGS WE SHOULD ALL THINK ABOUT

1. Cooperation is a requirement for improvement.

2. Do you think that the learning experience requires a sense of discipline, fear, and obedience?

3. What does it mean when we say, "Questioning reality is what constitutes being human"?

4. There is never a time in man's life that he should say, "I don't have to listen."

5. Morality is a code of conduct while ethics set the standards to follow. Is this taught in the Bible?

6. Do you agree that education influences the requirements of becoming a rational and an acceptable moral person?

7. Do you agree that it is religion and faith that forms the basis and the foundation for the creation of a moral person and society?

8. Knowledge is the foundation for the need for salvation and reconciliation.

9. Obedience to God brings blessings, but sin carries its own punishment.

10. Does one have to have a religious belief to be a person of character?

11. Have you thought about how you can make this world, your life, family, workplace better?

12. What does doing the right thing mean?

13. How many people like Joe Valery or Cathy do you know?

14. Why do you think the innocent have to suffer?

15. What kind of character do you project?

16. On that day when Jesus is waiting for you, what will he say? What will you say?

17. Heaven and life eternal may be a promise, but death is a reality.

From the Book of Sirach: Divine Wisdom
You led men and women to put into the Bible
words that would bring us closer to you,

Help us search the holy Scriptures better
each day. Enlighten us in these changing
times to acquire the wisdom and grace
to understand your call, reinterpreting
it for our contemporary lives while
remaining loyal to its eternal message.

Let your word, like good seed,

We ask this through Christ our Lord. Amen

| Chapter Three | *Everything Has A Beginning* |

The authors of Genesis—wrestling with the when, where, who, why, and how did I get here questions and why do the innocent suffer—must have concluded that man had been indeed assigned to pay a price for disobeying God's will, which was a result of the "thou shalt not" commandments and really meant "or else you may not only suffer but could even die."

Bertrand Russell said, "Ever since man became capable of free speculation, their actions in innumerable important respects have depended upon their theories as to the world and human life, as to what is good and what is evil. To understand an age or nation," he says, "we must understand its philosophy, and to understand its philosophy we must ourselves be in some degree, philosophers." **(1)** The point is, it is the circumstances of men's lives that do much to determine their philosophy, and conversely, their philosophy does much to determine their circumstances. In Genesis, the author shows us how man became part of the universe. Perhaps God is foreshadowing man's need for a philosophy called religion. Leo Tolstoy, in *A Confession* writes, "If Religion is the establishing of a relationship between man and the universe, then morality is the indication and explanation of those activities that automatically result when a person maintains one or other relationship to the universe . . . morality," he continues, "cannot be independent of religion, since it is not only a consequence of religion, that is, of the relationship a person has to the world—but it is also included in religion by implication. Every religion is an answer to the question of the meaning of life. And, the religious answer includes a certain moral demand." **(2)**

Adam and Eve had a moral and ethical obligation not to eat from the tree of knowledge. The problem was they did not know what this obligation meant nor what the real consequences of their actions would be, a true case for "the devil made me do it" defense. If morals are rules that guide behavior and thinking, don't we need to know what the result would be if we did or did not choose to obey the rules? All Adam and Eve had in Genesis is the talking snake appealing to the virtue of Eve's greed. "You'll have the same knowledge that God has," he said. "You do want that, don't you?" If there had been others who had experienced a similar situation for Adam and Eve to emulate or discuss the good and bad possibilities with, their choice may have been different.

A LOT OF DECISIONS ARE MADE BASED ON WHAT'S IN IT FOR ME. We have concluded so far that an ethical person promotes justice, displays compassion for others, is honest in his dealing with others, and shows respect for all of God's creation. Perhaps Adam and Eve came to the same conclusion that Einstein wrote in his letter to M. Berkowitz (October 25, 1950). Although he claimed not to be an atheist, he said, "My position concerning God is that of an agnostic, I am convinced that a vivid consciousness of the primary importance of moral principles for the betterment and ennoblement of life does not need the idea of a law-giver, especially a law-giver who works on the basis of reward and punishment." My question becomes, doesn't the learning experience require a sense of fear and obedience?

It probably was the Adam and Eve story in Genesis that inspired Karl Rahner in *Foundations of Christian Faith* to conclude that "man was created with the ability to transcend his limits and to experience a relationship with God. It is with this relationship that gives me the ability to encounter God in everyday life," and according to Rahner, "is what makes us human." **(3)**

"When man recognizes that he has limitations, for example, he begins to explore possible ways to go beyond those limitations. Striving to go beyond one's limitations," says Rahner, "presents choices and when we ask whether one choice is better than another, a decision is made and man learns to be responsible for that choice by acting freely."

For Rahner, explains Mark F. Fischer in his paraphrase of *Foundations*, "The ability to put reality into question is what constitutes the human being. Without a 'God,' who is the creator and sustainer of reality, there would be no one to question the meaning of reality, and the defining characteristic of the human would be absent. Humanity would no longer exist." Fisher goes on to say that Rahner believes that it is "our experience with others that enables us to know ourselves as the person whom we 'see' when we reflect on our experience of the world. The experience we have raises, in our minds, the question of who we are and what we ought to be. The freedom to act responsibly then, is essential to God's communication with human beings."

In chapter 3 of *Foundations*, Fisher interprets Rahner by saying, "It is with man's free actions that people achieve their life's work and define themselves. But human freedom is never complete because we always act within a context imposed by history; which is to say, we remain hearers of God's word, never the master of it." Rahner's view, according to Fisher, is that "the self-righteous person is always capable of rejecting God. Such people, he says, delude themselves into thinking that they are acting freely and responsibly, but may profess atheism in the name of human freedom, and thereby affirm God, albeit indirectly and inexplicitly. The mysterious God, who offers people freedom and invites them to act responsibly, just as he did in the Garden of Eden, remains the sole judge of the moral quality of their lives."

The accumulation of actions by man contributes to and forms his final achievement and according to Rahner with "every free act expresses our relation to God . . . and so in every free act we make a decision for or against God. However, because every free act is conditioned by factors beyond the individual's control, the human being can never be certain of the moral quality of his or her decisions. There is no point at which one can say, now I finally understand God's communication, and I no longer have to listen." It seems to me that maintaining obedience to God and our adherence to moral norms would require, as Rahner puts it, an "intrinsic unity between morality and religion." According to the Ten Commandments, and as pointed out in *Foundations*, "Love is the absolute sum of all moral obligations. If love is the genuine love of true religion," says Fisher, "then its expression is genuinely moral, and cannot be opposed to moral norms. The good we do, and the hope we have, are experienced in moral decisions; when we choose the good, we participate in the eternal life of God, the source of good." Fisher concludes that, "Christian faith affirms that the history of the world as a whole will in fact enter into eternal life with God. By contrast, the possibility of eternal loss (hell) is merely a possibility, not God's will." **(4)**

MORALITY AND ETHICS CREATED A RELIGION, but the link between morality and ethics seems to depend on what philosophy you are subscribing to and what issue you are addressing. It's reasonable to conclude, based on most of the interpretations available for consideration, that morality's most popular definition entails that which involves a code of conduct, while ethics generally attempts to dictate the standards to be followed when dealing with a particular act, such as business behavior, medical treatment, buying and selling transactions, etc. Ethics suggests what is a right or wrong way to do things. The question becomes, for whom do these concepts apply and on what basis? Do they apply to all individuals, to all groups, and to all the members of a particular society or profession?

Can the same moral code of conduct or behavior apply to various cultures and intellects on the same level? Didn't the intellect of those societies, which existed in the past, living in various locations of the world, differ from today's communities and groups who are currently in the same part of the world? It would seem to me that a society's code of conduct that would determine right from wrong for its citizens in the 1800 would conflict with today's counterpart simply because of its intended recipient's education, experience, and purpose. In New York and Chicago, for example, there are persons living in communities with every conceivable culture of the world who must live under one form of government. How would they correspond with, say those of a small Midwestern town in Oklahoma in 1939 versus 2008? I would suspect it would be an impossible task to get all individuals, in any one group, to accept the same code of conduct much less all members of all cultural groups to agree on one moral code of behavior. Because groups tend to define morality in an ambiguous way and are made up of individual behavioral attitudes, it seems it would be hopeless to expect everyone to adopt the same moral code.

Philosophers such as Immanuel Kant and John Stuart Mill for example, hold that morality is a code of conduct that all rational persons would put forward for governing the behavior of all moral agents. That sounds good, but now we have a different problem, what does a rational individual mean? Are Kant and Mill implying that if an adult living in any society is rational or normal, then it would be reasonable for them to know the kinds of actions permitted in a society of another culture? The rules of conduct or behavior, I should think, should be consistent, changing with the times, but maintaining the idea that morality would favor a code of conduct which promoted love over violence, peace over killing, endorse charitable actions over greed, and promote individuals living together in peace and harmony without justification for any action which would violate such standards. Was this the way it was in the Wild West of the 1800s in St. Louis, New Orleans, New York, Texas, or Kansas City? According to *The Natural Law Tradition*, from the Greeks to the present day, explicitly holds that all rational persons know what kinds of actions morality prohibits, requires, discourages, encourages, and allows. They also hold that reason endorses acting morally." **(5)**

Once again, it seems as though education also influences the requirements of a rational and normal, moral person. Those persons who have the knowledge and intellect required to understand the difference between good and evil and what actions will benefit the total group the most along with the ability to develop rules which reinforce the achievements of such desired acts such as prohibiting murder, stealing, inflicting pain on others, cheating a person, or making false statements to influence another will be the group that succeeds the most.

Do we define, as Bernard Gert concludes, "Morality is an informal public system applying to all rational persons governing behavior that affects others and has the lessening of evil or harm as its goal that when it is important that moral questions lead to disagreements and need to be settled, that societies use political and legal systems to supplement morality?" **(6)** He cites, for example, the question of whether it is moral to allow abortion, and if so, under what conditions? While the courts have pretty much handled this problem, not all individuals, especially the Catholic faithful, agree with the results. As another example, almost every Christian abhors the courts' rulings regarding the right to display the Ten Commandments on government-owned property or in front of the courthouses. Were these concerns apparent in 1776?

What Is the Role of Religion in a Moral Society? Thomas Walsh of the International Religious Foundation said it most convincingly in a speech he delivered at the International Coalition for Religious Freedom Conference on the subject of Religious Freedom and the New Millennium, "For the vast majority of people today the foundation of ordinary morality for most people is religion." He concludes by pointing out that it is the "stories of Jesus, Buda and Muhammad that have become the fundamental stories and narratives—the heroes and heroines that people want to model their lives after and that serve as the basis of their moral lives." Therefore, he continues, "Despite the unhappy aspects of the history of religion, religion has, in fact, been the fundamental basis of ordinary morality throughout the world."

On that basis, Mr. Walsh concludes, "There is a legitimate reason to say religious freedom does lend support to the idea of creating a moral society." (7) We can also say that it must be the freedom of religion that God gave us that promoted morality throughout the world. From *The Analects* of Confucius, "I practice three principles that are close to my heart: one is to be kind, two is to be frugal, and three is to be modest. Being kind, I have courage, being frugal, I can be generous, and being modest, I can lead. These days people abandon kindness for mere bravado, abandon frugality for extravagance, and abandon modesty for power and control, all of these being disasters." (8)

The principles of morality, as discussed by Kant, Mill, and others—along with the teaching of the religious faiths such as Christians, Jews, and Muslims—all give support to the idea that moral standards regulate right and wrong conduct and that by living with a moral standard, a code of conduct which teaches that good will overcome evil, and a morality that will teach us that ethics, which is the culmination of these principles into a manual of good conduct, will determine what actions are good for the betterment of the community regardless of the time.

Today we seem to have developed a disagreement of what constitutes ethical behavior. In Kenneth R. Melchin's work, *Living with Other People*, he writes, "Debates over issues give rise to debates over theories, methods, principles, and approaches. Eventually, he says, the very meanings of the words, ethical, moral, right, and wrong are called into question." (9) Everyone has their own opinion and "every interest group promotes its own agenda in the name of rights. Whose rights take priority?" Good leadership is the foundation of an ethical society. Melchin makes a very interesting correlation between Christian faith and moral and ethical behavior. He says, "Salvation is deliverance from the reign of sin and evil. Thus a discussion of the debilitating effects of evil introduces the role of Christian faith in moral knowing and acting." (10) I think it is interesting that the creation of knowledge,

which was born from evil sin, becomes then the foundation for the need
for salvation and reconciliation, which can only come from God. The
need for religion, which comes from our belief in God, shall determine,
therefore, a moral requirement that we develop a code of conduct that
requires a loving relationship with God. Sin, which is portrayed as the
significant result of disobeying God's will in the Genesis story, plays an
important role—to be sure—in the development of man's future; but it
seems to be sin, because of knowledge, which generates a completely
new challenge for man's mind to deal with cautiously. It seems to me
that the results the Genesis writer was trying to achieve was to show why
a society needs to demonstrate a lifestyle that promotes morality that
is loyal to God's will. The fact that a society needs to demonstrate an
acceptable morality based on a universally developed ethic of honesty
and loyalty is why its philosophy was created.

The theme of serving and obeying the Lord is emphasized throughout
the Bible and seems always to point out that obedience to God will bring
blessings, but sin carries its own punishments. Moses paid the price
for not obeying our Lord even though he was chosen by God to be the
leader of His chosen people. This should make the point clear to us that
even though the Lord names love as the reason He freed His people
from the bondage of slavery, He says, "You will suffer for your sins
and know what it is like to have me against you" (Num. 14:34). The
people eventually went back to their old ways even though the Lord had
told them before they entered the promise land to "be strong and very
courageous. Be careful to obey all the law my servant Moses gave you.
Do not turn from it to the right or to the left, that you may be successful
wherever you go. Do not let this Book of the Law depart from your mouth;
meditate on it day and night, so that you may be careful to do everything
written in it. Then you will be prosperous and successful. Have I not
commanded you? Be Strong and courageous. Do not be terrified; do not
be discouraged, for the Lord your God will be with you wherever you
go" (Josh. 1:6-9). Again, the theme of fearing the Lord and serving the
Lord is repeated at Joshua 24:14-15, "Now fear the Lord and serve him
with all faithfulness. Throw away the gods your forefathers worshiped
beyond the river and in Egypt, and serve the Lord. But if serving the
Lord seems undesirable to you, then choose for yourselves this day
whom you will serve, whether the gods your forefathers served beyond
the river, or the gods of the Amorites, in whose land you are living, But

as for me and my household, we will serve the Lord." **(11)** I think it can be said that the first rule a society should make is a commitment to be for or against God.

HOW THINGS WORK: Making better decisions requires the establishment of a theology, which accepts, loves, and worships one God. Whether we are making decisions involving organizational policies, career moves, personal relationships, or participating in all sorts of community planning projects, we are required to be more sensitive to the presence of and acceptance by an ever-increasing multicultural society. Arriving at answers or suggesting solutions to the simplest of problems requires a more disciplined thinking process than ever before. The complexity in satisfying so many different cultures, each with a different set of values and traditions, presents a tremendous challenge for planners and decision makers. Even the task of raising a family in today's world that features a relaxed morality, high technology, and poor societal ethics has become more difficult for parents of all faiths and backgrounds than ever before. Massive government spending, high unemployment and the demands of competing in a global market contribute greatly to the frustrations felt by individuals, communities, and businesses around the world.

Attempting to solve problems proficiently and being able to deal effectively in a highly technologically driven society requires more people skills than ever before, along with an analytically and logically organized mind. It has become rather obvious to me, if the leaders in our society are going to reach adequate conclusions to the problems facing the progress of communities today, the successful plan will have to reflect and deal with a variety of multicultural opinions, customs, and historical traditions. If we are to make good decisions today, we need to have an appreciation for the lessons of the past so that what was good can be repeated and what was bad can be avoided. Additionally, knowing how to compromise and still satisfy the objective would be a very valuable lesson to learn. Yesterday's realities, which are facts that have already been experienced, take on an important role in making future decisions. Hoping that the future will be better than the past requires a confidence on the part of decision makers that must permeate onto the majority of the group's membership and depends on the persuasiveness of the project leader in order to receive a majority consensus.

If we expect to create sound, moral, and ethical leaders tomorrow, we need to become role models and mentors for our students, friends, colleagues, and neighbors today. To do this, we will need to improve our own thinking as well as promote a concentrated effort to change the thinking of those in our society who only seem to respect individuals with status, instead of recognizing a person's character, those who welcome others from other cultures only if they recognize a family's historical background instead of welcoming newcomers from other cultures as persons with fresh ideas, and finally, those who are interested in preserving the current self-serving establishment rather than showing support for those with a different point of view who have a real penchant for a better tomorrow for all. We will also have to realize that it is only with a spirit of cooperation that we will be able to successfully improve our society and the men and women in it. Realizing how important it is to share our talents and listen to new ideas instead of being bias and uncooperative will help us to become more successful in our efforts to build a more united and stable society. If the result that is achieved by authorities and citizens is common to all, this end is called the common good.

As we continue to develop new ways to challenge our thinking and create ways to accomplish our goals with the good of the community in mind, we just might change a negative attitude into a positive one. Further, by being conscious of our need to be charitable, perhaps we can encourage the homeless to find ways to increase their spiritual awareness, in hopes they will increase their self-esteem and build a better image of themselves. In short, by explaining what human rights are and how to earn them, by promoting peace and love with our neighbors, and by listening with the intent to be helpful instead of critical, we can begin to change an attitude of resentment and discouragement into one of cooperation and respect. When one feels that there is a genuine concern for one's problems and that an honest effort to find a workable solution is being made to solve them, attitudes will change and disagreements are compromised.

WHY WE ACT LIKE WE DO: People must understand the spirit in which things were founded and developed before they can be better prepared to understand what part they will play in its future, particularly religion. For example, Egypt's society, politics, and economic systems were elite; but their religion embraced mythology. Each dynasty (family who ruled) related to the world with their polytheistic beliefs. Many of the ancient artworks depict gods, goddesses, and pharaohs who were considered divine. The pharaohs' power was almighty and unquestioned. Christianity and Islam were not practiced in Egypt until the Graeco-Roman era. It was after the Greek conquest of Egypt under Alexander the Great in about 330 BC that Egypt's culture expanded. Alexander appointed Greeks to all the major positions of authority and founded Alexandria. The Greek influence lasted nine hundred years but in 30 BC, after the death of Cleopatra, Egypt's last queen, the Greek influence was incorporated into the Roman Empire. Egypt was then ruled from Rome and then by Constantinople until the Persian and Arab conquests.

Under the Greek influence, hieroglyphics was replaced with the Greek alphabet thereby making the study of religion open to just about everyone; however, under Nero, the Roman government imprisoned, tortured, and made the Christians fight wild animals for entertainment. The Christians kept their faith by remembering Jesus's words that those who suffered persecution because of his name were truly blessed. Eventually, Christianity won the battle and had penetrated the highest levels of society. It was in Egypt that Christians openly worshipped in defiance of the Romans. As the Romans struck down one church and martyred the Christians, more would be converted and other churches built, when Constantine became one of the Roman Empire's emperors, the persecution of the Christians ended. In 313 A.D., a policy of religious tolerance throughout the Empire was put in place, and for the first time, a social peace fell over the land. Christianity was made the official state religion under Constantine's Edict of Milan and able to stand up to the mighty Roman Empire. Egyptian civilization proved to be one of the greatest and longest lived in the ancient world. Today, this civilization and its unique history and mysteries consisting of pyramids, mummies, art, great temples, and the life-giving flow of the Nile are known and visited by peoples of all nations. The Egyptians were God's first successful Christian society.

Looking back in history, it wasn't until the medieval ages, around the twelfth century, that urban society started to grow. Those who were tradesmen and artisans, looking for a greater number of customers, contributed initially to this growth. Retail merchants and administrative workers followed and soon the urban community was diversified and offering a wide variety of goods and services. To make sure the community continued to grow and continued to offer equal opportunities to newcomers, rights and responsibilities had to be written and structured into rules. Regulations and enforcement procedures had to be created that would assure that the rules and an acceptable code of conduct could be carried out properly. As the population grew, the government became burdened with the task of keeping enough revenue available to provide administrative services, social prestige, and could offer more opportunities to its citizens. You get the picture!

As long as the economy was good, all went well, but when the economy declined, it became more difficult for the community leaders to provide adequate services. It was also difficult for urban leaders, in the early societies, to accomplish an atmosphere of similar interests and values. The rules and regulations had to be enforced in such a way that acceptable behavior would result. Effective oral and written communications, as well as a tolerance for a moral behavior which reflected cultural differences, had to be established. An ethical behavior that recognized differences in the social and religious attitudes of the people had to be become standard practice. Allowances for individual behavior patterns had to be developed because it was important that these standard ethical practices be recognized by that culture as acceptable practices. The authority therefore had to permit some degree of flexibility and a certain amount of compromise in order to reflect the thoughts and practices of a multicultural group for their variances in what was to be called standard social, political, and religious freedoms.

As the population became more culturally mixed, it became more difficult to keep the interest in the community united. Today, because of history, we can form a clear picture of how it could have been, with how it is, and determine why it is not as it should be. Ultimately, however, when one engages in war for the sole purpose of establishing and enforcing a particular lifestyle on a group of people who hates everything their opponents believes, who wins in the end? During the years that witnessed America, struggling to become the America it is today, military leaders, politicians, scholars, and theologians attempted to influence the thinking of the majority of its citizens by appealing to their sense of values. Their respect for the society in which they lived, their ethics, their moral laws that they received from God, and their faith in their religious practices help to guide them to try and find a positive solution less devastating than war. However, to the godless, war was the only weapon, which, in their mind, would accomplish the goal of overcoming a dictator. The American Revolution was found to be the only apparent way to rid the new United States of the British king's tyranny.

SOCIETY SHOULD RESPECT THE DIGNITY OF ITS CITIZENS: It seems to me, in order to become a more productive and efficient member of a society, we need to start by answering the question of what influenced our lack of progress to become more productive and efficient in the first place. It is important to understand the role citizen's play and what characteristics are prevalent in causing their successes and failures. We know, for example, that when the prevailing attitude among society's leaders is self-serving and reflects a lack of concern or respect for the common good, its people will become resentful and will eventually look for alternative lifestyles. A society that shows little respect for the dignity of its citizens usually creates, within that community, a spirit of mutual disrespect between the people and its leaders. This attitude breads animosity, unrest, and ignites problems that only gangs try to remedy. Those decision makers, on the other hand, who genuinely work to promote a spirit of cooperation, compromise, and show a real concern for the common good, usually find it much easier to produce solutions that are acceptable to all. How a society is organized in terms of its laws and policies, its economy, and the political atmosphere it projects directly affects the opportunities for its citizens to grow. "The moral test of a society is how it treats its most vulnerable members. When we recognize that all people have a right to participate in the economic, political, and cultural life of their community peace becomes the fruit of the justice which is created." **(11)**

This atmosphere is again a utopia, because, for most of us, Christian behavior is at the core of our actions but for the Jew or Muslim who cannot accept that Jesus Christ is necessary in their life, a moral and ethical code is required to make sense to them as well as to others. I have often wondered about the cry for help by the Christian Jews in Egypt when Moses delivered them from bondage because "I heard the cries of my people" as compared with the Jews, some of whom I'm sure were Christian Jews, who were put to death by the thousands in the Nazi concentration camps. I'm sure their prayers were just as desperate as the Egyptians, but were they unanswered because of their rejection of Jesus? There were some saved when the Russian and American army liberated the remaining prisoners. Are the Jews of today, who do not accept Jesus, confined to the law as written and interpreted in the Pentateuch, the first five books of the Bible, for their salvation? God's chosen people who were saved by God sending Moses to free them from the evils of the Egyptians is the same God who sent his son to save and deliver us from evil and promises that whomever believes in Him shall have everlasting life.

Since the beginning of man, religions have molded the world into what it is today, and I think it will be the religion of today that will be practiced tomorrow that will keep man in God's favor. God's grace will allow all men to continue to learn how to handle that which has been recorded in the Old and New Testaments.

THERE WAS A PRICE PAID FOR FREEDOM: Our founding fathers certainly knew that the common thread weaving its way through the fabric of our history that gave morality its significance was religious freedom. All of history has recognized religious freedom as being the basic foundation that makes a society moral, and when we add political and educational freedom to our list, we have combined the magic ingredients that can best establish a peaceful and compassionate behavior to our society. It is and always has been these three freedoms that help us focus on knowing right from wrong and how to promote those decisions that benefit the common good. Although I share the view of those philosophers and historians who hold that the universal characteristics of morality and politics, bonded by the values which each holds, do change with time from society to society, it seems obvious to me that the most consistent characteristic motivating us toward an acceptable morality is indeed our freedom of religion, education, and politics.

When one makes a comparison of the many important historical events in recorded history with the most memorable stories from the Old Testament Bible, one thing is very clear: the leaders of the nations with the greatest amount of wealth maintained the largest well-trained army.

Throughout time, it has been man's economic power and military might that has been the ultimate weapons in acquiring that which was desired. The history of Egypt, for example, beginning in 3000 BC involved one battle after another; however, it was the "Gift of the Nile," as it was called by the Greek historian Herodotus in the fifth century that made Egypt the major agricultural and cultural center of the eastern part of the Roman Empire. Economic power sometimes trumps military threats. However, whether it was the king's dynasty or military leadership, each victory experienced inflated the ego of the oppressor. As the successes continued to fuel a leader's desire and ambition for power, his attitude would project a greater arrogance and thirst for additional victories. The more victories he could amass, the more he reasoned he would be assuring his place in history as the leader of the greatest nation in history.

To him, rather than encouraging alternative ways of dealing with the problems each country was facing, military training took precedence over all other activity. Besides, it was easier to take what you wanted than to deal with enemies who were not interested in your compromises. It has been recorded throughout our history that the rise and fall of nations have found that men engaged in mortal combat with one another was the most popular method in their effort to find solutions to their problems. From the downfall of Mesopotamia to the early years of this century, man has been fighting man.

Our Declaration of Independence expresses the principles that people are entitled to certain rights that cannot be taken away by the government. The most important of these rights says that all men are created equal, that they are endowed by their Creator with certain inalienable rights, and that among these are life, liberty, and the pursuit of happiness. These ideals, which were written in 1776, are the cornerstone of our American government; but as the Declaration of Independence was being written, there were those, such as John Adams who, in a letter to his wife, wrote, "I am well aware of the toil, and blood, and treasure, that it will cost us to maintain this declaration and support and defend these States. Yet through all the gloom I can see the rays of ravishing light and glory." **(12)** The surrender at Yorktown in 1781 ended the first war in a new country. With the help of France and Spain, full independence from the British had been won.

All Military and Economic Dominance Comes with a Price: Zachary
Karabell in his work, *Peace Be Upon You* writes that there are many stories
that were part of the Jewish tradition but, when told by Muhammad,
were different. "Moses, Noah, Jacob, and other biblical heroes figure
prominently in the Quran," but as Karabell explains, "while their stories
are largely the same as in the Torah, they are not precisely the same. And
that in itself opened a fissure between Muhammad and the Jews." **(13)**
A significant reason for this difference stems from the period of time
between the events' occurrence to the time it was written: the gospels
were written within seventy years of the death of Jesus but the biographies
of Muhammad came more than two centuries after his death. Referred
to as the "People of the Book" (the Bible) Jews and Christians like the
Muslims were chosen by God to receive his message. The problem,
according to Karabell was, even though "the message that Allah delivered
to the Hebrew prophets and then to Jesus was pure, but according to the
Quran and Muslim tradition, in the process of transcribing what God
had said, Jews got the stories and the morals wrong and Christians erred
in thinking of Jesus as the Son of God rather than that of a prophet
and the Son of Mary . . . for Muslims the great failing of the people of
the Book was that they had distorted the message." **(14)** "Because the
Jews and Christians were so intimately linked to Islam," writes Karabell,
"Jews, Muslims, and Christians, due to shared traditions, could all be
considered 'People of the Book.' They were all members of a family, he
says, a family created by God. And just as a brother cannot kill his brother
no matter how misguided that brother is, Muslims had to find a way to
tolerate Christians and Jews, no matter how lost, foolish, and sinful they
were." Within two years of Muhammad's death, writes Karabell, most
of the Arabian peninsula belonged to Arabia and within ten years the
Arabs had conquered the territory now belonging to Egypt, Israel, Syria,
Lebanon, Jordan, Iraq, Southern Turkey, Western Iran, and the Arabian
Peninsula. The interesting result of the Islam's military conquests is that
Jews and Christians lived in peace with the Muslims but they had to pay
a poll tax, which allowed them to govern themselves, worship freely,
and select their own leaders. They could not have armies nor have any
control over any city or province, notes Karabell. Whereas Judaism and
Christianity began as a religion of small groups, Islam developed as the
religion of an expanding empire. Within a hundred years of Mohammed's
death in 632 AD, military conquest extended the Islamic world to India,
North Africa, and Southern Spain. **(15)**

Building a better life for all to enjoy comes with time but also has its price to pay. There is a saying I heard in a movie that said, "When you give a mouse a cookie he wants a glass of milk." Over the many centuries, what really has changed? We all seem to want that glass of milk. In the 1960s, President Lyndon Johnson, for example, had big plans for the United States and wanted its citizens to wage a "War on Poverty." Among the things Johnson felt every American should be provided was an education for every child and some type of health care for all, and finally, there should be an end to racial discrimination. Sound familiar? Medicare was born for the elderly and still provides benefits today. The Elementary and Secondary Education Act gave school districts over $1 billion in federal funds for needy students. Today, we're still trying to throw money at education to solve its problems but have now additionally mandated that every school district in the country adhere to the rules of "No Child Left Behind," which has its own downfalls; but most importantly, this legislation is causing teachers to teach to pass tests.

In the late '50s, a housing act was created and continues today in the form of "Habitat for Humanity," providing housing for low-income citizens. Then in the name of humanity came more war when we were called to protect the South from the North in Vietnam. Consider these facts: Vietnam was the longest U.S. war. It began in 1965 and ended in 1973 for the United States. In 1975, the North Vietnam Army captured Saigon, which was the South Vietnam capital. Over 58,000 Americans were killed with the total cost to the United States over $150,000 billion. This war caused confusion about the nation's role in world affairs and society treated its returning veterans with very little respect. Are we still losing lives, spending money trying to fix everything, and wondering what is right in the name of helping protect the repressed? Do we still want a universal health care, an end to discrimination, and maintain the attitude that more money needs to be put into our school system to solve its problems? Last week, our local paper reported that there were over 114,000 citizens that could not read in our county. The local news reported that more girls between thirteen and nineteen than ever before were pregnant. Sin, created from knowledge, wars, greed, disrespect for humanity, slavery, discrimination, doubt in God, injustices, and a lack of self-respect has caused us to be where we are.

In chapter 3 of John Steinbeck's epic novel *East of Eden*, Adam Trask's father, Cyrus, is explaining the nature of a soldier to his son, "I'll have you know that a soldier is the most holy of all humans because he is the most tested—most tested of all," he says. "I'll try to tell you. Look now—in all of history men have been taught that killing of man is an evil thing not too be countenanced. Any man who kills must be destroyed because this is a great sin, maybe the worst sin we know. And then we take a soldier and put murder in his hands and we say to him, use it well, use it wisely. We put no checks on him. Go out and kill as many of a certain kind or classification of your brothers as you can. And we will reward you for it because it is a violation of your early training." Then comes the ultimate question, Adam asks, "Why do they have to do it?" **(16)** Why is it? WHY IS IT, indeed.

THE RIGHT DECISIONS ARE NOT ALWAYS EASY: Throughout the Bible, there are stories of the experiences of man making decisions and their outcome. During the growing years of our great America, these stories served as an important reference source and example of how to make better decisions. A very important factor and influencing decisions became man's loyalty and devotion to his "family." Without question, the family became the moral strength of society. The progression of the importance of family values, as man's most important virtue, became a leading factor in the development of a more acceptable social behavior and foreshadowed the future behavior and importance of families for generations. Family values were right on up there with repenting sins when it came to the subject of preachers' sermons during the early growth and development of the Western frontier.

While these subjects were the two most important subjects for preacher's sermons during the early years of America by the 1960s a declaration of individuality and a desire for freedom was developing. Materialism, technology, and war were condemned. Between then and the 1980s, the conservative movement in the United States grew in strength. Through the years, we have seen how socially and morally our society seems to change, like the wind weaving between what's right and moral and what's only in individual man's best interest. During the 1980s a popular movement called the moral majority became prominent. Its leaders included young preachers named Jerry Falwell, Jim Bakker, Oral Roberts, Jimmy Swaggart, and Pat Robinson who were Evangelical and Fundamentalist Christians. They interpreted the Bible literally and believed in absolute standards of right and wrong. They condemned liberal attitudes and behaviors and argued for a restoration of traditional moral values. They worked to reduce the nation's high divorce rate, lower the number of out-of-wedlock births, encouraged individual responsibility, and generally tried to revive traditional values.

Of these five men, however, Jerry Farwell and Pat Robinson are the only ones who have escaped embarrassment because of their life choices. Jim Bakker went to jail for his involvement in a scheme to raise millions of dollars for a theme park that never happened and lost his marriage due to infidelity. Jimmy Swaggart confessed to having an affair during the time he was married, and Oral Roberts built a huge hospital, which was destined to fail from the beginning, later retired, and left his son Richard in charge. Richard was asked to resign because of allocations that he was spending school money on his personal lifestyle, draining the college his father Oral built of its finances. Fortunately, a very wealthy businessman saved the college by offering to donate an amount equal to what the university needed if Richard would retire and had nothing more to do with the school. When I think about the many conflicts caused by man's greed and the efforts of those with compassionate concern for the social conditions of hunger, disease, and poverty, I'm reminded of what Kenneth Melchin in his book, *Living with Other People*, concluded, "Whatever we may think about the social challenges of our age, the fact remains, that the course of human history is still in God's hands." **(17)**

DOES GOD WANT YOU TO BE RICH? A few weeks ago, our high school librarian was giving away past issues of *Time*, *Newsweek*, and other magazines. While looking through some of the offerings, I found an article written for *Time* by David Van Biema and Jeff Chu entitled "Does God Want You to Be Rich?" Curiously, I began reading. "One of God's top priorities is to shower blessings on Christians in this lifetime," was the message George Adams drove deep into his memory banks and is what inspired him to become a top car salesman instead of an out-of-work, used-to-be, successful forty-three-year-old. He believed, "God wants to support us. It's Joel Osteen's ministry that told me. Why would an awesome and mighty God want anything less for his children?"

"Prosperity Theology," the authors wrote, "known under a variety of names—Word of Faith, Health and Wealth, Name it and Claim It, has its emphasis on God's promised generosity in this life and the ability of believers to claim it for themselves." They continued, "In a nutshell, it suggests that a God who loves you does not want you to be broke. Its signature verse could be John 10:10, 'I have come that they may have life, and that they may have it more abundantly.'" There seems to be some controversy in this message, however, from others who do not bear the same message. "That God's goodness is biblical, as is the idea that he means us to enjoy the material world is half right," say the critics. "But while Prosperity claims to be celebrating that goodness, the critics see it as treating God as a celestial ATM." While Joel Osteen's prosperity-driven mega church, Lakewood in Houston, is telling people they will prosper, Rick Warren of *The Purpose Driven Life* says, "This idea that God wants everybody to be wealthy is baloney . . . You don't measure your self-worth by your net worth. I can show you millions of faithful followers of Christ who live in poverty. Why isn't everyone in the church a millionaire," he asks. Joyce Meyer, another popular TV preacher of the Prosperity Lite camp, according to the article asks, "Who would you want to get in on something where you're miserable, poor, broke, and ugly and you have to muddle through until you get to heaven?" **(18)**

I don't think God cares if we have all the nice things money can buy or whether we give all our money to a mega church, claiming what it can do for us in return, or whether we support TV pastors in fine clothes decorated with diamond rings and gold chains who ramble on about how they think we will get to heaven. Without God's love, there wouldn't be a church; without God's sacrifice of his son on the cross and his ascension into heaven, there would be no Christian religion; and without the teachings of Jesus while he walked among us, there would be no Christian teachings to follow. God wants us to know Jesus, to study his teachings, and to do God's will, which is to live our life using His commandments as our guide. While he is waiting for you, he wants you to fulfill His plan for you, whatever that may be—doing right above all else. Prayer, faith, and trust in God are the ingredients that will cause God to shine His grace upon you—not how much you give for love offering or contributions to mega churches. The peace and love within you will make you rich, maybe not financially but certainly spiritually, and your promised reward will be from Jesus not the evangelical or Pentecostal church that preaches great rewards for your donations. I am glad that Mr. Adams was inspired to do what he was capable of doing in the first place but did so because he attended Mr. Osteen's church. If he would have asked God for His help, he could have accomplished and found what he was looking for. Blessings come to us, not in the church or from societal pleasures, but from God and a respect for the dignity of our human self. If it takes mega churches, theatrical performances with lights, music, and promises to inspire us, so be it, but give the credit to God, not pastors with fine things, silver-tongued words, and alligator shoes.

The fantasies created by some of the followers of the "Prosperity Evangelists" remind me of the conclusions a group of friends and I would reach while brainstorming about things that usually had no realistic answers, only theoretical opinions. For example, I remember a discussion we had regarding the *Oracles of Nostradamus* by Charles A. Ward. Nostradamus, you might recall, wrote prophetic verses in 1554; however, no one could understand their meaning until after the event he had predicted occurred and the oracle was restudied. Nostradamus was a very learned man. He received his MD at the age of twenty-six and proved to be way ahead of his time in the field of medicine. He was a scholar of languages and studied astrology. It was said that he had even predicted his own death. When his assistant wished him a good night on July 1, 1566, he was reported as saying to him, "You will not find me alive at sunrise." He was found dead on July 2, 1566.

After long discussions about how he had the ability to make such accurate predictions, which included the death of Marie Antoinette, we concluded that he must have traveled or lived in the future and simply recorded what he remembered about the experiences he saw when he returned to his own time. How could he know that there would be great fire birds flying out of the east that caused the end of the world? Since space has no time, the fourth dimension theory, we analyzed, could apply. Did this mean, we wondered, even though we were sitting around the table drinking coffee now, could we be in the middle of a super highway sometime in the future?

As I remember, some of our more challenging discussions had a religious connection. One afternoon we were discussing the role of religion in the progression of society. History, we said, along with oral tradition which had been edited over the years because of newly discovered information along with editorials, parables, debates, discussions, poetry, and myths, all taught a lesson most of which often seemed to have a religious theme for us to think about. As the population matured, we concluded three things had to happen and did in most cases:

- The society disappeared because of the greed and ambitions of its leaders;

- improved due to the cause and effect of education, religious motivation, and respect for human dignity; or

- grew due to a code of conduct based on a God-based, religious moral behavior, a respect for human dignity, and living by the decisions made in the best interest of the common good.

Fantasies are not realistic and promises made by those who cannot make them come true are like our theories, they can only be created by our creative imagination. A person in need of help emotionally, financially, or spiritually can be easily influenced by the promises of the Prosperity preachers. They will tell us what we should believe and why we should believe it, how we should live our life, and if we send a love offering, we will receive their latest book, bible, prayer card, and blessing as a gift. These people place a high priority on the need for their listening flock to send contributions in order for their ministry to continue, which is true of any religion. But we, on the other hand, hear only the promise of what we will receive as our reward for sending a contribution. Donations for the support of the ministry are the theme preached by most of them, but they are becoming rich in the process while their vulnerable listeners begin to doubt their personal degree of faith because they have not received the promised blessing of earthly riches. Prosperity Evangelists enjoy private jets, large estates, enormous incomes, and lifestyles way beyond one's belief. According to newspaper articles, several are currently under investigation by the IRS for not paying the proper amount of tax on the amounts they are receiving.

These religious evangelists and their methods are also being noticed by big businesses. For example, consider what a four-hundred-pound guy named Jared did for the Subway sandwich! His promotions, which show him eating Subway sandwiches and successfully losing weight, produce support for the product. Jared becomes what is known as a "product evangelist" and his followers, who are anxious to receive the same weight-loss results as he has, enjoyed eating Subway sandwiches and became "customer evangelists" with every pound they lose. As a result, Jared and Subway made lots of money. This is the same principle that the television evangelists use. They have made evangelists of those who support their message by word of mouth, telling potential worshippers about the sensational programs they can participate in, the awesome music, tremendous choirs, and once in a while, a celebrity appears. Why do things work that way?

In the name of religion, wars have been fought, promoters of various schemes have embezzled millions of dollars, donations have been used for personal gain, and lives have been ruined because of greed and extramarital sexual involvements. Despite it all, the reality is, there seems to be more and more who want to join in the preachers' cause. My feeling is that there is obviously something missing in these types of followers' life that they have to look for sensationalism and entertainment in their theology. And for those who are promoting rewards for financial support, who are motivated to encourage others to participate solely to support their personal recognition, in my opinion, are doing an injustice to their believers. A Dr. Laura writes, "The essence of religion is not just to have an emotional and mystical feeling about heaven and God but to understand that there are expectations and obligations from God to direct our lives toward goodness." (19) It seems to me that we should learn to recognize the difference between possessions that make us feel accomplished and those that make us feel spiritually peaceful.

When we face diversity with prayer, we can live with the choices we make much easier knowing that our conclusions were influenced by God's grace and compassion. It has been my theory that the recipe for a happier and successful life comes from the ability to make good decisions. We can do this by asking for God's help to reach those goals we have realistically set for ourselves and by living a life based on a code of conduct based on His will. Wouldn't it be wonderful if we could project a spirit of confidence, a respect for human dignity, a strong work ethic, and principles of a Christian moral attitude in our character? By instilling in others this kind of confidence in our everyday life's activity, people would not have to guess what our position was going to be and that the common good would be served.

BE RESPONSIBLE: All of us have heard our parents, teachers, preachers, and everyone else who has ever had a serious discussion with us expound on how we need to be responsible for the choices we make. God holds us responsible for how we live our lives, so why shouldn't parents, teachers, preachers, and society hold us responsible for our choices? Anything less would not honor us as human beings, would it? The catch is, they cannot tell us how to make those choices, and we seem to be people who would rather be told the answer than to work it out for ourselves. I'm not talking about those decisions such as what movie should I see—although for some young folks that could involve outside guidance, just like the Internet does today—or what am I going to wear, but rather, those decisions that require thought and will usually involve the feelings or require some kind of action on the part of others. Since I am a firm believer in the proposition that learning should be a thing that improves the efficiency of one's mind, I would rather learn how to handle problems before I have to face them. This is why I enjoy reading novels, Bible study, and history so much.

The problems of others can become mind without the pain, which is inflicted by making the wrong choices. When the decisions I have to make require more immediate answers, I will usually talk with others who have had the same problem and seek their advice, or I might explore ways in which the same problem has been dealt with by others. Life-changing decisions require more council; therefore, I will certainly ask for divine guidance before weighing all the pros and cons of my choice. If a decision requires technical skills, factual information, or instructions are readily available. When it is in a book, the problem can be resolved quickly. The unfortunate part about decisions that involve some of the day-to-day activities we experience—such as awkward situations that come up at the office, school, or when social situations arise—answers can't be found in a textbook and require a magic ingredient that a lot of people just don't have called COMMON

SENSE. One cannot teach common sense to another but one can certainly learn how to reason and analyze things out by using moral and ethical principles as a guide.

Regarding major decisions, I think it is important to consider what responsibilities the choices and decisions will require and be assured that they will have the willingness and fortitude to complete those responsibilities. They also need to calculate, with some degree of forethought, whether their choices and decisions, if implemented, will produce the results needed. Thirdly, I think solutions concerning groups of people, such as situations involving our schools, church, civic organizations, and local governments should be made with the best interest of the common good in mind instead of favoring those with biased and self-serving interests. Finally, when an individual, group, or a newspaper editorial expresses a point of view relative to a subject that is controversial, it is important for interested persons to present their position on the same subject so that alternate positions and solutions can contribute to the process of compromise and produce greater flexibility, which will compliment a greater range of possibilities.

EVER SINCE THE BEGINNING, the knowledge of what's right and what's wrong has determined man's moral development. Before Mom and Dad was guiding us, it was a talking snake appealing to our desires for something we weren't suppose to have but promising great things if we'd take the next step and break God's "will" that was influencing us.

Ever since the beginning, we have tended to do what is easier. Societies of the past made bad decisions because they lacked a moral framework. Like Eve, people want more than they have; they want to "fit in." Because of this, their decisions are usually based on what will make them, in the eyes of others, think they are "cool."

As our world grew older, so did our moral framework—just as children grow to be adults, their character got stronger. They were learning what was good from evil. Even though mistakes were made, people of faith learned to resist temptation and how to conquer adversity. We have been challenged every day since the beginning to trust in God and live by his "will."

Our integrity grows when we are honest, and we become a person of our word. When this happens, people learn to rely on our commitment to do what's right. They learn to trust that we are responsible and develop a confidence in us that we will do what we say we will do. Every day is a new beginning. We are challenged every day to learn what happens when the spiritual order is broken and what to do to make it "just right"!

THINGS WE SHOULD ALL THINK ABOUT

1. Every religion has answers to the question of the meaning of life. In addition, the religious answer includes a certain moral demand.

2. Doesn't the learning experience require a sense of fear and obedience?

3. Making good decisions today requires us to have an appreciation for the lessons of the past.

4. A society that shows little respect for the dignity of its citizens usually creates, within that community, a spirit of mutual disrespect between the people and its leaders.

5. To be strong and courageous is a message from God.

6. Do not let yourself become discourage; this requires faith and trust in God's promise that he will be with you wherever you go (Josh. 1:6-9).

7. The first rule we need to make in our life is to make a commitment to love and serve our Lord.

8. Your family should be your most valuable asset.

9. All of history has recognized that it is religious freedom that is the basic foundation that makes a society moral. When political and educational freedom are added, we have combined the magic ingredients that can best establish a peaceful and compassionate behavior in our society. It, therefore, seems to me that we should learn to recognize the difference between possessions that make us feel accomplished, those that make us feel spiritually peaceful, and how—when we face diversity with dignity and grace—we can live with the choices we make much easier. God holds us responsible for how we live our lives, so why shouldn't we be held responsible for our choices?

10. Bertrand Russell once said, "On the banks of the river of Time, the sad procession of human generations is marching slowly to the grave; in the quiet country of the Past the march is ended, the tired wanderers rest, and all their weeping is hushed." *

11. Jesus said, "If you make my word your home you will indeed be my disciples, you will learn the truth and the truth will make you free" (John 8:32).

12. Our faith is a gift from God, given to us as a result of knowledge.

Chapter Four	*Where And Who Is God?*

During one of my pastoral ministry classes at the Newman University, I was given a handout by our instructor entitled "What Is God" by Danny Dutton, age eight. The article was captioned, "This is quite possibly the most enlightening article you may ever read on this subject—written by an eight year-old!" I have no idea where my instructor got the article or whether Danny is a real person, whether he really wrote it, or if it was done by a ghostwriter. The point is, I enjoyed it so much that I wanted to share it with you by including it here as an introduction to this chapter. I hope Danny would approve!

What is God, by Danny Dutton

One of God's main jobs is making people. He makes these to put in place of the ones that die so there will be enough people to take care of things here on earth. He doesn't make grownups. Just babies. I think because they are smaller and easier to make. That way He doesn't have to take up His valuable time teaching them to walk and talk. He can just leave that up to the mothers and fathers. I think it worked out pretty good.

God's second most important job is listening to prayers. An awful lot of this goes on, as some people, like (priests) and things, pray other times besides bedtime. God doesn't have time to listen to the radio or TV on account of this. As He hears everything, not only prayers, there must be a terrible lot of noise going into His ears, unless He has thought of a way to turn it off.

God sees everything and hears everything and is everywhere. Which keeps Him pretty busy. So you shouldn't go wasting His time by going over your parents' head and ask for something they said you couldn't have.

Atheists are people who don't believe in God. I don't think there are any in (my town). At least there aren't any who come to our church.

Jesus is God's Son. He used to do all the hard work like walking on water and doing miracles and trying to teach people about God who didn't want to learn. They finally got tired of Him preaching to them and they crucified Him. But He was good and kind like His Father and He told His Father that they didn't know what they were doing and to forgive them and God said OK. His Dad (God) appreciated everything He has done and all His hard work on earth, so He told Him He didn't have to go out on the road anymore. He could stay in Heaven.

So He did. And now He helps His Dad out by listening to everyone's prayers. You can pray anytime you want and they are sure to hear you because they've got it worked out so one of them is on duty all the time. You should always go to Sunday school because it makes God happy, and if there's anybody you want to make happy, it's God. Don't skip Sunday School to do something you think will be more fun like going to the beach. That is wrong. And besides the sun doesn't come out at the beach until noon.

If you don't believe in God, you will be very lonely, because your parents can't go everywhere with you like to camp, but God can. It's good to know He's around when you're scared of the dark or when you can't swim very good and you get thrown in real deep water by big kids. But you shouldn't just always think of what God can do for you. I figure God put me here and He can take me back anytime He pleases. And that's why I believe in God.

Thank you, Danny, for your thoughts!

Over the years, I have listened to several debates regarding whether or not God existed, and I always came away feeling sad for those who denied His existence. In *The Sources of Modern Atheism*, it is written, "God is no longer a habitual concern for human beings. Less and less do they call him to mind as they go through their days or make their decisions . . . God has been replaced by other values, income, and productivity. He may once have been regarded as the source of meaning for all human activities, but today he has been relegated to the secret dungeons of history . . . God has disappeared from the consciousness of human beings." **(1)**

Today's world seems to have sent God on his way, but we need to recall John 5:36, which tells us that the works of Jesus is a testimony that God sent Jesus to do the works of God. These works are the evidence of faith in God and are performed to bring glory to God rather than man. The good works that Jesus performed was the product of the grace of God. "In times past, God spoke in partial and various ways to our ancestors through the prophets; in these last days, he spoke to us through a son, whom he made heir of all things and through whom he created the universe" (Heb. 1:1-2). God in the Old Testament gave us all the proof a reasonable person should need for his existence, but man continued to disappoint him. The New Testament tells us God sent his son in the flesh so people could see, hear, and touch him. Hebrews continues in 11-1, "Faith is the realization of what is hoped for and evidence of things not seen." Atheists who read, *The Sources of Modern Atheism* should heed the warning made to all Christians in the Letter of Jude, "a slave of Jesus Christ and brother of James wish to remind you, although you know all things, that the Lord who once saved a people from the land of Egypt later destroyed those who did not believe." (Jude 1: 5)

History has taught us that everything which has a beginning shall have an ending, and the Bible teaches us that the criterion for the "judgment of nations" will be the deeds of mercy that have been done for the least of Jesus's brothers. Matthew writes, "When the Son of Man comes in his glory, and all the angels with him, he will sit upon his glorious throne, and all the nations will be assembled before him. And he will separate them one from another, as a shepherd separates the sheep from the goats. He will place the sheep on his right and the goats on his left. Then the king will say to those on his right, 'Come, you who are blessed by my Father, Inherit the kingdom prepared for you from the foundation of the world. For I was hungry and you gave me food, I was thirsty and you gave me drink, A stranger and you welcomed me, naked and you clothed me, ill and you cared for me, in prison and you visited me.' Then the righteous will answer him and say, 'Lord, when did we see you hungry and feed you or thirsty and give you drink? When did we see you a stranger and welcome you, or naked and clothe you? When did we see you ill or in prison, and visit you?' And the king will say to them in reply, 'Amen, I say to you what-ever you did for one of these least brothers of mine, you did for me.' Then he will say to those on his left, 'Depart from me, you accursed, into the eternal fire prepared for the devil and his angels. For I was hungry and you gave me no food, I was thirsty and you gave me no drink, a stranger and you gave me no welcome, naked and you gave me no clothing, ill and in prison, and you did not care for me.' Then they will answer and say, 'Lord, when did we see you hungry or thirsty or a stranger or naked or ill or in prison, and not minister to your needs?' He will answer them, 'Amen. I say to you, what you did not do for one of these least ones, you did not do for me.' And these will go off to eternal punishment but the righteous to eternal life" (Matt. 25:31-46). Will you be on the right like the sheep or on the left like the goats?

HOW DOES ONE KNOW WHAT TO DO? There comes a time in everyone's life, regardless of age, when we must make some serious decisions. When this happens, we may feel we have been given too many burdens to deal with and begin to question our role in life, our faith, relationships, and everything and everyone who seemed to be contributing to our frustrations. In times like these, we usually retreat to a favorite place to think about things, or we seek the wisdom of someone we trust to tell our woes. Listening to someone we trust can either be very helpful or can make things worse. Friends, for example, sometimes tend to be too honest and cause us not to want to accept the truth.

When I was a teenager, I remember how important it was for me to have a place to go to think when faced with important problems. Being a country boy, that usually was either in the haystacks of the barn or in the forests on my horse; someone to talk to was usually my dog who was always by my side. I know there are things that concern teens today that are different from my concerns and that young adults may not experience the same kinds of problems as teenagers do; but I suspect they do have concerns that require thought, help from a friend, or a need to know where to find answers. But what if there is no place to go, or no one to talk to?

As a teacher, one of the goals I tried to accomplish was to give young people a plan to follow that would help them deal with problems. As I thought about how to do this, I remembered the lessons I learned in Sunday school and how our teacher would make them seem relevant to the times and the problems we were experiencing. I remember discussing Bible stories and how much fun it was to share ideas with her and my classmates about the lessons Jesus was trying to teach by the parable he told. Like so many today, people either don't understand, understand but choose to do something else, or learn well and live their life according to God's will.

I wanted to teach my classes something meaningful, something that they would remember for a lifetime. I wanted to teach them a method to use that would help them make important decisions, help them to diagram a plan of action that they would remember, and to teach them principles that would help them maintain a character envied by all. I hoped what we did in class would create memories for them. I hoped what we talked about would mean something to them, not only now, but later in life; something they could recall when answers to important questions were required, when their decisions, if implemented, would affect others, and when they were called upon to make important decisions. I wanted them to remember those things we had discussed that would, sometime in their future, help them.

One year, I thought about having a court trial with the students playing the part of attorneys, the jury, witnesses, experts, and other important persons, etc. The question to be considered was going to involve the death of Julius Caesar and whether or not the death of Julius Caesar was murder or justifiable homicide. The first assignment, after we read the play, was to go to the public library and read the critics' interpretations. They had to research the history of the times politically and economically, learn some things about the author that could have possibly influenced the content of the play, analyze the characters, what the political mode at the time had to do with the plot to kill Caesar, and anything else which would support their position—such as the social and religious attitude of the community, the cultural influences, etc. Next, they should write an outline that included a description of the problems that influenced the act, what they thought caused the act, and what kind of persons were involved. They were also asked to include what they thought a dream solution would be, explaining how their solution would be in the best interest of the common good, what effect it would have on the community now and in the future, how the major characters would be affected now and in the future, and the steps they would take to accomplish their conclusion. The outline would look something like the following and the instructions would say:

> Keep in mind you are making your case from these points.
>
> Present a well-defined explanation of the problems facing the people during the time of Caesar. Include information on whether the economy was good or bad, what were the political questions, and how did the social and religious attitude of the community influence the conspirator's conclusions.
>
> What problems existed that caused the conspirators to consider killing Caesar? What action on the part of Caesar caused these problems? Quotes should be used from the play to support your answers.
>
> (When using research information, please identify your source and use appropriate quotes to support your statements.)
>
> Who or what caused the community to think the way they did about Caesar? (Use quotes to support your conclusions and thoughts.) Who in your opinion caused the problems?
>
> What does the play say about friendship? Research the characters: who they are, what role they played in the government, in the community, in the death of Caesar, etc.
>
> What were the feelings of the community before and after the death of Caesar? What did the conspirators hope to accomplish for the future by killing Caesar?
>
> How do you think the problem should have been resolved? Guilty or innocent? Was the death of Caesar necessary? Was getting rid of Caesar in the best interest of the community?

Why or why not? Was Caesar unreasonable? Is your solution realistic? Why?

What does each member of your team have to convince the jury in order for your solution to be acceptable?

What resources do you need to make your solution a reality? In other words, what does the community have to do, or how must they change in order to make your solution believable? What compromises must the government make with the people?

What would your solutions be? Explain how they would be in the best interest of the community.

The trial was a big success. Everyone participated and enjoyed what I thought was a real learning experience. My secret hope (long-term goal of the project) was that students would use the same methods in finding solutions to future problems they might have as they did while they were preparing their case.

When I was a teenager—and even later—at the ripe old age of twenty-two, I couldn't seem to find the answer I needed to solve what I considered to be an important problem, at least not the kind of answer that made me feel confident about the conclusion I had reached. It was frustrating, especially when I realized what little resources I had to help me reach an acceptable solution. A "How to Procedure Guide" was what I wanted to come up with for my students' consideration. I wanted to be careful, not to lecture, but rather suggest. By using literature, history, and common sense as a guide, I hoped to teach them a procedure to follow that might help them make better decisions. Any important problem I thought needed to be defined and understood before a solution could be found. For this reason, I recommended they write an outline that defined the problem and what they thought had caused it, who the major characters were, who they thought caused the problem, and who they thought they could count on to have a sympathetic ear or provide some help in finding a solution. All the players needed to be identified. From a group of selected novels and short stories, I selected those who concentrated on realistic plots with believable characters that they could relate to and study how the problems were handled. The character traits of the protagonist were studied, and we concentrated on how his relationship to the other characters made the story realistic. It would also, I thought, be helpful to think about what other acceptable solutions could have been developed.

Rewriting scenes or endings became an exercise in solving problems. Next, we would analyze whether that solution was realistic or not, if the solution made sense, and why the character would do what he did or was made by them to do. Depending on the story, times in history, or the conditions—economically and politically—it was determined whether the resources to make the solution workable could easily be made available or achievable. For example, better organization of time: did more money have to be earned, how could life have been better, did a tragedy influence the outcome, how could it have been avoided, character flaws and what caused them, etc. By this point, they should either feel confident that they could work out simple problems and learned how to handle larger ones, or if it was concluded that the problem had no immediate solution, it would be better to wait until the resources needed could be acquired first so that a better result could be accomplished. This would be especially true if their list of resources for a workable solution required more money or a car. The danger was in real life that if a solution seemed hopeless now, a slide into depression could occur and thoughts could turn to "I have no money and getting a car is out of the question. What to do?" In their frustration and feeling of hopelessness, "theft" may cross their mind, in which case, the door would be opened for making bad choices. The problem is now becoming like a cancer, spreading to the point of making bad choices, which is now being fueled by an "It's not fair" syndrome, which is an attitude that only serves to make a bad choice seem justified. This is the kind of scenario that a combination of circumstances can create and exactly the kind of situation I wanted them to be able to recognize and learn how to avoid. If by recognizing that these events can happen by the way the character reacted in the novel or story, I was hoping they would see the wisdom in accepting an alternative solution or have the patience to wait for a time when they could do something more realistic to solve their problem instead of following the path of the character who chose crime or some other unacceptable solution.

At the right time, I would tell students a story of how an army friend of mind decided to handle a very important problem. The story took place around the time in history when black students were trying to break the bounds of discrimination. Most had learned about the Rosa Parks incident, but not about the struggle blacks had being admitted to white universities in the South. In 1962, two people were killed and seventy-five were injured in rioting at the University of Mississippi because James H. Meredith attempted to break racial discrimination by being the first black man to go to the university. One day, as my friend and I were discussing this terrible problem, my friend said to me, "I'm going to go to a good northern college so that I can get an education and receive my BA. These people," he said, "who are trying to break the discrimination barrier in the south can't study or concentrate under those conditions. After I receive my degree, I'll go to law school and after that, I'll run for the U.S. Congress. When I am elected, then I can do something constructive for my fellow black citizens by working to change the law so that they will have an equal opportunity to learn." He concluded, "By receiving an education, they can become an asset to society and not a statistic." To me, my friend had the right idea. Not long afterward, the landmark Civil Rights Act of 1964 and the Voting Rights Act of 1965 outlawed racial discrimination, removed obstacles to voting, and furthered desegregation.

Several years later, I was teaching a Christian education class at my church, and I could tell that I had a special class. They were eager to learn, did their lessons faithfully, and participated in class with enthusiasm. After we finish studying the beatitudes, we talked about God's covenant with Moses and the Ten Commandments. Some of the kids thought it would be cool to write a personal covenant that they could live by; so like the trail of Julius Caesar, a project was started. We decided to make our own personal covenant. The purpose and ultimate goal of the covenant required students to think about and come up with a set of standards (rules to follow as they were growing up) that they would try to live by now and as they grew older. When the covenant was completed, each class member signed his/her classmate's copy as a reminder that the project was a joint effort. Each student received a special binder containing his copy of the covenant and in the back of the folder were some of their own competed homework assignments to review later in life.

The covenant read as follows:

INTRODUCTION

The undersigned students of our Christian Education Class have decided to make a life's covenant between us, as individuals, and all whom we shall know and meet during our lifetime. These standards of behavior will help us stay close to God and guide us when we are required to make life choices.

We have decided to make this covenant because we know God has given us a freewill and that all through our life we will be expected to choose between right and wrong. We know that we must be the one to accept the responsibility for saying, yes or no to God.

We believe God created us free to think, to choose, and to love. We are free to be faithful to God and to live according to his loving will for us; therefore, we do hereby present our life's covenant:

OUR PURPOSE

We intend to make mutual vows of loyal and mutual obligations to our current and future brothers and sisters so they will know that our life will be dedicated and empowered to do God's will.

We hope to become models of how God would want us to walk humbly with him. To do this and to help us make right choices, we will pray for God's guidance.

When we sin, we know that God will forgive us no matter what we do, if we are truly sorry and try not to sin again.

STANDARDS WE WILL STRIVE TO FOLLOW

We shall always take the following steps in our effort to make the right choice; as Jesus required His disciples to practice the spirit of love, mercy, peace, generosity, and justice, we pledge, in our covenant, to abide by that which Jesus taught in the beatitudes by remembering the following:

- How you act is more important than what you have.

- That sadness and comfort are part of life—you should be there for those who need you.

- To be patient, see the beauty in life, and appreciate what God has created.

- To do the right thing when required to make a decision.

- To be kind and helpful to one another.

- We will not let evil things be bottled up inside of us.

- We will put our selfish interest aside and help others to resolve their conflicts.

- To stand up for what is right.

- We will take time to think about what we are about to do before we act.

- We will ask God to guide us and give us the courage to make the right choice.

- We will look at all the possible choices and the effects each will have if implemented.

- We will think about which choice shows that we love God and others.

- We will say NO to the choices that will hurt others or us.

- We will go to others for help when we need advice or when it is hard to do the right thing.

- We will always try to choose the right thing.

OUR PLEDGE

Our council members pledge to respect one another and the dignity of others that we will meet along life's path. We agree to make, as our moral and social guide, the will of God as stated in the Law of Love and the Ten Commandments. We believe, by taking God's commandments seriously and putting God first in our life, that we can make a lasting contribution to the well-being of ourselves and others. In the end, we recognize that the virtues of faith, hope, and love will endure with the greatest virtue being love. We will say yes to this covenant by living responsibly. We know doing God's loving will is our best way to live in true freedom. Living by the first commandment means that we will put all our faith in God and choose to keep him first in our lives because we know when God is the most important thing in our lives, that we will live in freedom and will be able to work to bring about his kingdom, his reign of justice, and peace for all.

BY THE AUTHORITY OF OUR FAITH IN GOD AND HIS LOVE FOR US, WE HAVE HEREUNTO

SIGNED THIS COVENANT: _____
                              Student member of this Council

(Each student sign the other's covenant so they would remember that it was a group project and have the names of those who was in the class.)

I have no idea how many still have their covenant available to read. Some have moved away and now go to different churches. I can only hope that the experience of writing this covenant was a life-learning project that created memories for these young students. Like characters in a novel, all of them will face many situations in life, which will require them to make choices. They will be tempted, and I can only pray they will break the bonds of evil and restore hope in their life when hope has been lost. I feel confident that they will live up to their covenant.

When we are called on to make a choice between good and evil (or what we know is not right) the decision should be straightforward because evil is simply the refusal to do what we all know to be good, but evil challenges our ideas of justice and order—i.e., "I think I deserve it" attitude. Ultimately, it requires that we take a stand on the very foundations of hope itself and forces us to face squarely the implications of our basic convictions regarding our values. More than anything else, evil forces us into the realm of religious questions. This is when we need to call on our faith to restore our commitment to moral knowing and acting which is being eroded by evil. When we choose good, we are saying yes to Christ and those we love. It is the refusal to return hate when we are hated, the refusal to strike back when we have been cheated, and the refusal to give up on ourselves when things seem to work against us. When we choose the good, we do not work alone because the saving work of Christ's love refuses to let us fight evil with evil. This is what I hope my students learned from their Sunday school and public school experience.

Good versus Evil:

The first three chapters of the book of Genesis contains some of the most thought-provoking information regarding good and evil that man has had to deal with since knowledge gave him the ability to make choices. Every individual since Adam and Eve has been plagued with the struggle between choosing between good and evil.

Therefore, it happened.

"God looked at everything he had made and he found it very good. Evening came and morning followed—The Sixth day." The seventh day was holy and he rested.

But the serpent convinced Eve to eat from the tree of knowledge of good and evil. Eve in turned convinced Adam to eat. Hence, evil became a by-product of man's lack of faith, trust, and obedience to the Word of God.

"EAT FROM THE TREE OF KNOWLEDGE, THE TREE OF GOOD AND EVIL."

Evil is a privation, that is, it needs special conditions to be present in order to produce its effect. When you think about it, if God wanted to create a perfect world for man to live in, such as the Garden of Eden, why do you suppose he would put man into a situation that would require him to make a choice between disobedience and faithfulness? Could it be that we must first know what evil is and what its consequences are before we can know what good is?

When asked why Adam ate from the tree, his immediate reaction was to blame Eve as he responded, "The woman whom you put here with me—she gave me fruit from the tree so I ate it." Then Eve blamed the serpent, when she was asked she replied, "The serpent tricked me into it, so I ate it." Does this pattern sound familiar? Everyone is so quick to blame someone else for his or her actions. As a matter of fact, most arguments consist of accusations: who did what to whom and why! Most of us try to build a defense of innocence, but the results are usually no better than the serpent that was banned from all the animals and from the wild creatures and made to crawl on his belly and eat dirt. The woman didn't fair too well either; to the woman, he said, "I will intensify the pangs of your childbearing, in pain shall you bring forth children. And finally, to the man, he said, "Because you listened to your wife and ate from the tree of which I had forbidden you to eat, 'cursed be the ground because of you! In toil, shall you eat its yield all the days of your life?'" (Gen. 3:17). His punishment continues at Genesis 3:19 as God says, "By the sweat of your face shall you get bread to eat, Until you return to the ground from which you were taken, For you are dirt, and to dirt you shall return. Then the Lord God banished him from the Garden of Eden, to till the ground from which he had been taken. When he expelled the man, he settled him east of the Garden of Eden." Thus, the mystery of suffering was born. The author further suggests that the first culture and society was created with the birth of Cain and Abel. Cain was a tiller of the soil and Abel became a keeper of flocks. When the Lord became more pleased with an offering of one of the best firstlings of Abel's flock, Cain became jealous. The Lord tried to tell Cain not to be resentful but rather to hold up his head if he thought he did well otherwise sin would lurk at his doorstep.

If our purpose as humans is to do good works and glorify the name of God, then it seems to me that evil would not exist if we lived in an environment where our love for God was so strong that temptation could not overcome us. If we are allowed to choose unfaithfulness and disrespect for God's wishes, however, then evil will exist because we have removed ourselves, at least temporarily, from His love. On the other hand, maybe the author of the Genesis story is trying to explain to his audience that there needs to be order in the universe, a God-loving spiritual order, one in which people must follow in order to prosper but if disobeyed, suffering and eventual death would result. The tree of life and knowledge would therefore be the author's prop, a symbol representing God's Word, and the eating of the apple would represent sin, which is the breaking of God's order. The story teaches that in order for us to know that faith requires a strong commitment to be loyal to what one believes to be morally correct then we need to know what the alternative to faith would bring in order to understand the effect of evil. If sin is the lack of God's love, then sin is evil. But if our love for God is always going to be challenged and tested by making us make choices that could cause us to disrespect His wish in favor of satisfying our curiosity or desires, then evil is a moral and ethical problem. This action does not preclude that we do not love God. It simply means we have become a victim of sin.

The author of Genesis used, for example, the serpent to foreshadow the omnipotence of evil in man's future when he let man choose contempt and disrespect for God's wishes by eating the fruit from the tree of knowledge. Adam and Eve still loved God, so their act was a moral sin instead of an evil sin, which is the absence of God's love. Evil sin, therefore, may be classified as a spiritual disease that seeks out everyone. Our only defense against its powerful influences comes only from God's love. Through His gift of love, His divine grace, we are taught the lesson of His redemptive powers, but it took Jesus to teach us about reconciliation. The creation, life, and plight of Adam and Eve became the way the author of Genesis chose to explain how man went astray and caused life to become the challenge it was for the citizens of his day. What better way could the author have pictured heaven than being like a wonderful garden where one could walk and talk with God. A place so beautiful and pure that only a snake could mess things up and cause things to be out of control. What better way to represent temptation, shame, greed, and lust by using a beautiful tree bearing perfect fruits. The author teaches us that knowledge has its price, which is evil sin (represented by eating the apple) and moral sin (represented by Adam and Eve's decision to break God's spiritual order) and that man's dignity and ethics have now been compromised by Adam and Eve due to their lack of trust and faith in the Word of God.

Man's future character and integrity was now going to be dependent on the choices man would make. How ironic to learn that it was sin that increased man's knowledge of evil and that very process is what creates more choices. The ultimate significance of his choices was going to either improve or destroy the future worthiness of man and his relationship with God even though, in that process, some choices will cause him to sin as it now became his challenge to create a better society. The question he had to wrestle with was going to be whether or not the birth of sin was going to be an inherited thing that all of mankind would have to contend with, in other words, do the innocent suffer too or did God give us the freedom to overcome evil?

The story of Adam and Eve, it has been suggested, was written to explain to the people of the time the reasons for suffering and how sin causes a separation from God and not a story with a cause and effect moral. Adam represents all men, with the talking snake playing the part of the villain, and the tree of knowledge that of good and evil, which represents the order that God created these events. But what happens when this spiritual order is broken? Most scholars hold that the creation stories and the Adam and Eve stories are written in the myth genre. The subjects are so astonishing that it is hard to comprehend God saying words to create our universe and everything in it, but we are here in this wide wonderful world, which is experiencing the reality of its mysteries and wonders but not really understanding how its origin exists in all its magnificence.

WHY DO THE INNOCENT SUFFER? A teenage boy wonders why his sixteen-year-old girlfriend and best friend was killed in an auto accident. A New Orleans family wonders why their friend, who lost her home in the Katrina storm was killed in a tornado just before she had a chance to move into her new home; and a small boy wonders, with tears in his eyes, why Daddy is not coming home for his birthday party. How does one deal with these kinds of reality? Suffering is the reality we hope will bypass us during our life but seldom does. Suffering is when we fall to our knees and pray for the thousands of innocent victims who had to die because of wars, storms, fires, explosions, or other evil deeds. Suffering without cause is beyond our comprehension but is a certain reality of our life's experience.

"I am the Lord your God," it seems to me is one of the themes of Genesis while the other is, "The Lord is faithful to his promises." The snake's persistence that Eve eat from the tree of knowledge, to me, foreshadows our preoccupation today with a lust to be famous, rich, or more elite than others. We all have idols, which represent milestones that we will never reach but want. We all seem, sometime or another in our life, to have that secret wish or obvious craving to be like someone whom we could never be or have that something which realistically we know we will never process. The snake's insistence that Eve disobey the Lord's instructions so that she could be as intelligent, famous, and worldly as the Creator could seems to be a prophecy of the need for the second commandment, "Thou Shall not make unto thee a graven image." In other words, materialistic things should not be held in a higher esteem than God.

The Genesis author seems to be answering the question, "If man does not know sin, how will God's plan for salvation and penitence be accomplished?" He seems to be making a case for giving us knowledge, and he certainly is suggesting that there is a real responsibility that comes with its possession. For eternity, man would be required to make decisions. Man would need to accumulate as much "knowledge" as he could in order to make decisions, not just for his benefit, but also the societies in which he would live. God's creation had been given the ability to choose good or evil and to expect personal advantages. In other words, man could now factor in his expected gain while making decisions, but he also learned that "sin or evil" was an option not an automatic choice.

Another important lesson is foreshadowed here as well when he learned that with free will the advantages of making choices can produce results that are unexpected; therefore, man should not hold God responsible for any results not anticipated and never take "His" name in vain when things go wrong.

The Bible is one of God's ways of communicating with us. No matter how difficult it is to understand what God wants us to learn, knowing what you are reading is paramount to understanding its theme or message. The Bible is a collection of books, each one written with a different literary form called genres. When we engage in conversation, we must consider the subject, realize that people will have different opinions about the subject, and during our readings while discussing the subject, various examples will be used to support a conclusion. The parties to the conversation will tell others what the results of the conversation was and the details leading up to the conversation. These results in a style called oral tradition. Someone who was there passes the information on to others who were not present when the event took place. This style differs from the historical style in that the events were not recorded. For example, a baseball game has a written record of everyone who participated in the game and what the results of the action were. Fifty years from now, the game's participants and how they performed, as well as the outcome, will be as it actually occurred. When we read the Bible, we know that there has to be two causes at work—God and the writer. It will be the writer that God selects that will tell the story his way. He will have, and use, his own style; therefore, each story has to be evaluated differently.

If we accept that the scripture is divinely written, it is words that must express the story's meaning. As Father Kenneth G. Morman says, words are a "human invention—they have great power, but they are also bound by human limitations. They are often inadequate (how we struggle to express ourselves), they are bound to a particular period of history (changing nuance and even meaning over time), and most serious of all, they are born of human experience and as a consequence are utterly incapable of doing justice to what is properly divine, infinitely beyond human experience. The fact that the words of God in the scriptures inspired the writers cannot change this fundamental reality; they are inspired "human" words, and therefore have all the limitations intrinsic to human words. In the study of the scriptures, he continues, "One must be careful not to substitute our own wisdom for the Lord's deciding in advance how we want God to have proceeded and then staunchly refusing to consider any other possibility." **(2)**

"Words," adds Dr. Laura Schlessinger, "have a tremendous potential impact upon situations and people.—they can convey compassion and encouragement, blessings, and love; or, they can kill spirits and relationships." **(3)** Father Morman reminds us that "modern mainline/ academic scripture scholarship in no way denies nor even weakens our deeply held belief that the Scriptures are wholly and entirely, with all their parts, the true Words of God."**(4)** "For just as from the heavens the rain and snow come down and do not return there till they have watered the earth making it fertile and fruitful . . . so shall my word be that goes forth from my mouth—it shall not return to me void, but shall do my will, achieving the end for which I sent it" (Isa. 55:10-11). If you accept that the Bible is God's way of communicating with us, then it is very important that one study the scriptures with an eye on learning what God wanted to communicate and the style that the human author used to present it to us, and that takes study. Determining God's meaning, by what he divinely inspired the writer of the day to put in words for him to communicate to the people, requires the use of every academic means available.

Father Morman tells us that "mainline biblical theologians (scripture scholars) hold that a two-step process must be followed: First, it must be determined what the original author meant to teach his/her community by what he/she wrote, and then secondly, it must be determined what the implications of that message are for God's people today." He says, "Some may resist this conclusion, because it seems to imply that in order to really understand the Scriptures it is necessary to study formally, and this some are unable or unwilling to do." By way of analogy, he continues, "Even without a knowledge of Italian or without being familiar with the plot of the opera, 'Madam Butterfly,' an aria such as 'un Bel Di' can still be enjoyed as glorious music—but how much more does the listener derive from this same aria when they also know its setting, what is going on—the beautiful music still remains exactly like before, but now the knowledge of the tragedy that is building for the unsuspecting young Japanese woman who sings so movingly of her confidence in the faithless American husband, gives to this music a pathos that causes the heart to swell, heightening one's enjoyment of the music tremendously. In the same way, the Lord can use the Scriptures to speak to the heart of the most unlettered person; but how much more can the Lord do with someone who studies the Scriptures with every resource at their disposal?" **(5)**

Whether the scriptures have as their source, historical evidence, oral tradition, or a new discovery, the author's viewpoint may be presented in the form of a parable, debate or discussion, poetry, or myth. Whatever the genre, they all teach a lesson and have a religious theme for us to think about, ponder, or experience. If the author has used a myth to emphasize that, which is otherwise incomprehensible such as infinity for example, it does not take very long for us to realize that we cannot even imagine an end. As people grow in knowledge, so do their societies, causing their achievements to be greater for the good of all, disastrous because of evil intentions, or morally stronger because the people realized that they must change their ways. A story told as a myth will no doubt use symbols to represent what we know as realities. For example, the book of Revelations (also known as Apocalyptic) writers use symbolic language, much like the prophets, to draw the reader's attention to their characters present behavior and warning them of the future ramifications of an unchanged lifestyle. While apocalyptic writing talks about the future, it is really about the present. Examples of this type of writing include the book of Daniel (OT) and the book of Revelation (NT). As Margaret Ralph puts it, "It's apocalyptic literature which is written to people who are suffering from persecution. The intent of the author is to assure his audience that the God of history is in control of the present situation so that one need not fear, the persecution will end and good will triumph over evil."**(6)** Ralph, in the foreword of her book, *And God Said What*, illustrates the importance of knowing what the author wants to tell his audience by describing an incident involving the great American humorist, who poked fun at herself as a homemaker when she claimed that dryers ate socks. "Everyone who uses a dryer knows what she meant," says Ralph. "If a person from another culture were unacquainted with a dryer and did not know the literary form in which Erma Bombeck wrote, he or she might miss the intent of the writer and misunderstand entirely." **(7)**

Sometime during our lifetime, I am sure all of us have given a fair amount of thought about the cards we have been dealt in life, what we can expect in the future, why we have been given so many burdens to live with, and what happens when we die. Friends, spouses, or children may never know what our deep down thoughts on these subjects are nor will they know how they are affecting our life. If we do feel a need to share our feelings with anyone, it usually turns out that the person we want to share our information with is more interested in his own problems than ours. Someone who is teaching or preaching a specific theory of their own beliefs can hardly pay attention, with any degree of sincerity, to our thoughts, beliefs, or problems. If we really need or want help, it is easy to be hooked on the emotional appeals of a television evangelist. He will tell us what we should believe and why we should believe it, how we should live our life and, if we send a love offering of $25 or more, he'll send us his latest book, bible, prayer card, and or blessings as a gift.

TV and radio evangelists place a high priority on the need for their listening flock to send contributions in order for their ministry to continue. We, on the other hand, hear only the promise of what we will receive as our reward for sending a contribution. Donations for the support of the ministry are the theme preached by most of them. Currently, however, most of these ministries who advocate what is called the Prosperity Gospel are making themselves rich while leaving their vulnerable listeners doubting their personal degree of faith because they have not received the promised blessing of earthly riches. These Prosperity Evangelists, as they are called, enjoy private jets, large estates, enormous incomes, and lifestyles way beyond one's belief. According to some newspapers, several are currently under investigation by the IRS for not paying the proper amount of tax on the amounts they are receiving.

These religious evangelists and their methods are also being noticed by big business. For example, look what 400 lb Jared did for the Subway sandwich! His promotions, which show him eating Subway sandwiches and successfully losing weight, produce support for the product. Jared becomes what is known as a Product Evangelist and his followers, who are anxious to receive the same weight lost results as he has eating Subway sandwiches, become customer evangelists with every pound they lose. As a result, Jared and Subway make lots of money. This is the same principle that the television evangelists use. They prosper because of those who support their message by word of mouth. They tell potential worshipers about the sensational programs they have the awesome music, tremendous choirs, and once in a while, a celebrity appears. Why do things work that way? In the name of religion, wars have been fought, promoters of various schemes have embezzled millions of dollars, donations have been used for personal gain, and lives have been ruined because of greed and extra-marital sexual involvements. Despite it all, the reality is, there seems to be more and more who want to join in the preachers' cause. My feeling is that there is obviously something missing in these types of followers' life that they have to look for sensationalism and entertainment in their theology. And for those who are promoting rewards for financial support who are motivated to encourage others to participate solely to support their potential for mightiness and their personal recognition, in my opinion, are doing an injustice to their believers. As Dr. Laura writes, "The essence of religion is not just to have an emotional and mystical feeling about heaven and God but to understand that there are expectations and obligations from God to direct our lives toward goodness."

The problem is, as I see it, we still do not get it. The questions, which influenced Eve to make the choice of disobeying our Lord's instruction, are the same questions that are causing us to wonder about life today. The problems may be more complicated, personal, and universal; but they produce the same results. Eve created the moral problem of, can I be trusted? and the ethical problem of blaming someone else for the results produced by choices we do not like. The absence of knowledge and experience did not stop her sense of curiosity and what she gained caused death for all of us. This was the price of sin.

THINGS WE SHOULD THINK ABOUT

(1) "You shouldn't just always think of what God can do for you."

(2) God said, "For just as from the heavens the rain and snow come down and do not return there till they have watered the earth making it fertile and fruitful, so shall my word be that goes forth from my mouth—it shall not return to me void, but shall do my will achieving the end for which I sent it" (Isa. 55:10-11).

(3) To study the Bible, one should follow a two-step method:
a. Determine what the subject matter is and what the author wants us to learn, and
b. Determine the implications of what the lesson's meaning is for us today.

(4) How would your creation story—your Adam and Eve story and your tree of knowledge story—be written? Was the evil one the snake?

(5) Christian reality requires faith! The founding fathers, some of which were Deists, believed if it was not realistic to believe then it wasn't true. Is truth only present when an act can be proven?

(6) Does religious questions demand a moral answer?
    For example: To believe in God and heaven requires faith but to know death requires nothing. Heaven is a promise, and death is a reality. Is evil a simple matter of choice, or can some evil be good or can some good come from evil? Do you believe that "no story has power, nor will it last, unless we feel in our heart that it is true and true of us."

(7) Facts to remember while reading the Bible are as follows: do you agree or disagree?

    Things to Consider about the Bible story:
        What is the story saying to us (theme and moral or a lesson)?

A story has a subject (plot). What is this story about?

Who is telling the story (point of view)?

When and where was it written (the time in history or setting)?

For whom was it written (the audience)? In other words, who did the author anticipate would be reading the story, and what did he think they would learn from it?

Who was the author? What do you know about him?

All of these things influence its meaning and ultimately its importance to us.

Knowledge of how to read the Bible is more important than reading the words.

(8)   We have the free will to choose right from wrong; therefore, we need to be responsible to God for our actions.

(9)   Living by the standards of the Golden Rule and the Ten Commandments help build a strong character. Do you agree or disagree?

(10) We must accept the responsibility for saying yes or no to God. Ask God for his help, pray.

<table>
<tr><td>

Chapter Five
</td><td>

A Case For Religious Education: Why Do I Need To Belong To A House Of Worship?
</td></tr>
</table>

When I first learned Jesus had said, "I am the way and the truth and the life, No one comes to the Father except through me" (John 14:6), I became concerned. I wondered how those who couldn't read or write were going to learn about Jesus. I was concerned for Jews, Muslims, Deists, Agnostics, Atheists, Buddhist, and the backwoods population. I was told that these people did not accept Jesus as the Son of God; therefore, they would never be accepted into the kingdom of God? Some of them, I found out later, didn't even believe in God. Did this mean they would be voiding their opportunity to experience God's love in heaven? I guess I should have included my Catholic, Quaker, and Mormon friends as well because, according to what some thought they believed, there was no hope for their salvation. I wondered, if what was right and wrong to believe belonged only to a few, what would have happened to me if my parents had not taught me anything about the Christian religion or saw to it that I was baptized? If I had not gone to church and Sunday school, would Jesus have loved me any less? How about Billy Graham, if he had been born in Arabia of Muslim parents would he have devoted his life to preaching Islam instead of Christianity? These were pretty tall concerns for someone who was just starting to learn about his Christian religion.

As a child, I had been taught to believe that "God so loved the world that He gave his only Son, so that everyone who believes in him might not perish but might have eternal life" (John 3:16), that the Ten Commandments was our moral guide, that the divine revelation is the source of our Christian Faith, that Jesus loved us so much that he died to give us a pardon from sin and death, and that the Golden Rule was the origin of ethics. Robert Sheard, in *An Introduction to Christian Belief*, wrote, "It was His divine revelation which fulfilled the covenant of everlasting life for those who believed." He also said about the revelation, "The very essence of revelation is the manifestation of God's unconditional love which challenges the believer to love others in like manner. Since the love of God is revealed in its fullest meaning in Jesus Christ and is not dependent upon our acceptance but rather is totally

127

unconditional, the implication is that I must love the Lord my God with all my heart and with all my soul; and with all my might and be faithful to that commitment if I am to experience any sense of self esteem of God's love for me."(1) That pretty much covered what I was taught.

Thomas P. Rausch, SJ, reassured my belief that God loves us whether we choose to accept his love or not when, talking about God, he said, God's "offer of Love is a standing offer which will never be withdrawn. God's manifestation of love is unconditional in that God's offer of love does not depend upon the human person's acceptance. One can accept or reject God's personal manifestation of love says Rausch, but the human person cannot undo its existence or totally control its influence." (2) God to me, as the creator of all things, was loving, almighty, jealous, demanding, and forgiving. For the moment at least, this was all I needed to know. As far as the nonbelievers were concerned, I was hoping that maybe Jesus, the apostles, or maybe St. Paul would hold special seminars sometime during the nonbelievers' afterlife, and if they passed the course, they would be accepted into the kingdom of heaven. Then I read what Jesus said in John 10:16-18,

> I have other sheep that do not belong to this fold. These also
> I must lead and they will hear my voice and there will be one
> flock, one shepherd. This is why the Father loves me, because
> I lay down my life in order to take it up again. No one takes
> it from me, but I lay it down on my own. I have power to lay
> it down and power to take it up again. This command I have
> received from my Father.

Could this be the passage that addressed my concerns, or was this passage a foreshadowing of what was to come? Wasn't Jesus sent by God to provide the human answer to the mystery of life, to show everyone the way, the light, and the truth?

It's interesting to note that even though no one can prove or disprove the existence of God the Jews and Muslims believe in the Christian God as being the only true God but only give Jesus credit for being a wise teacher and not the savior. It would seem to me that anyone with as strong a faith in God as they had could apply that same strong faith to believe that God had indeed sent His son to us, thereby fulfilling the prophecy of the coming of the Messiah as it was written in the Old Testament. I couldn't help think how the Old Testament showed that it was faith that brought the Christians to God, Mohammad who brought the Muslims closer to God, and Moses who brought the Jews to God; but didn't God in the New Testament bring Jesus to everyone?

God created, for each religion, what was to become their statements of beliefs. He guided the Jews to believe in the Pentateuch as their law, the Muslims to believe in the Koran, and the wise teachers to teach and lead the Hindu and Buddha believers how they should dedicate their lives. This being the case, wouldn't God expect them to be faithful to their religious beliefs and teachings? Wouldn't He expect them to believe that He was the only God in their life and that their theology, as it was revealed to them, was to be followed faithfully, regardless of what it was called? If God made all these people and gave them different religions, each with their own statements of beliefs, it seems to me that there should be a reason why Christianity was the only religion with a holy relationship with Jesus. What was the connection between Christians, Jews, and Muslims going to become? What part in the grand scheme of things were the Hindu and Buddha's going to play? Why would God make the world so complicated? Wouldn't it be important to learn about these three religions and beliefs, as well as our own, in order to understand the similarities between them. What was going to bring us together?

There was a pattern developing here; I knew I'd have to know all I could about what God expected of me before I could understand what He expected from others and what their relationship to me should be. Would studying other religions make my religion more meaningful to me or would I become very confused? The thought did cross my mind that maybe Jesus only applied to those who were called Christians, and only Christians should be concerned with His teachings as it was written in the Bible. These questions were going to require answers that I was not able to find an answer for at the moment; so I thought I'd better let God worry about the relationship between these people and Jesus and concern myself with learning everything I could about my Christian religion. In any event, I felt it was going to be important to keep an open mind when it came to the study of other religions. First, I had to learn more about my own. It seemed to me the place to start should be after Jesus's death, on Pentecost, when He revealed himself as the Holy Spirit and gave birth to the church. Without His divine revelation, which only God could have done, the Christian Church would not have been born and there would be no need for the Christian New Testament. Jesus brought the inspiration of the Holy Spirit to the bewildered apostles on this day. He knew they needed to strengthen their belief that they had the ability to build Jesus's church by preaching the gospel effectively and become successful fishers of men. The house of God, whether it is a church, mosque, or synagogue, is the house of the Lord. If God created man and everything on earth—including the creation of all faiths, philosophies, and religions—one would think that their followers would know what it mandated, follow its beliefs, and live by its moral and ethical standards just like the wise leaders of the Hindu and Buddha faithful require and expect the practice of their philosophy to be lived daily.

In the introduction to *Religions of the World*, we're told, "It is estimated that well over half the world's population practice, to a greater or lesser degree, one or other of the world's religions or indigenous spiritual traditions. They might be members of the largest religious community in the world, The Roman Catholic Church; which is a community of nearly one billion from every nation on earth, united by a shared faith and tradition, or, they might be members of a community whose number small but where faith is central to their lives, such as the Druze of Lebanon, whose form of Islam is so secret that the inner teachings are known only to those born into its community."**(3)** It may be that salvation may very well depend on how well one has followed his religious beliefs, whether or not it includes a belief in Jesus to be the Son of God or not, as long as God is the only God and the one they worship. If such belief and devotion to God is strong enough and His theology studied and believed strongly enough to be practiced faithfully, every day, then it should not be a challenge to believe that Jesus is the Son of God with whom He is well pleased.

Passing on Traditions: After Pope Paul VI wrote Dei Verbum, known as the Dogmatic Constitution on Divine Revelation, Bishop Paul, Servant of the Servants of God, together with the fathers of the sacred council for everlasting memory, wrote in the preface to the divine revelation that "this present Council wishes to set forth authentic doctrine on divine revelation and how it is handed on, so that by hearing the message of salvation the whole world may believe, by believing it may hope, and by hoping it may love." **(4)** I thought the act of God revealing himself to his apostles through Jesus Christ, even though it may be accepted or rejected, was an act of God that is not a matter for debate but a supreme event in history. It is my prayer that these dedicated scholars continue their work under divine inspiration so that the whole world will truly grow stronger in their attempt to believe, hope, and love.

Where Does Our Religious Experiences Come From? Like most young people, what I knew about the life and teachings of Jesus came from the birthplace of my knowledge: my parents, broaden somewhat by Sunday school teachers. Although this was as it should be, the truth is, most youngsters have not acquired very much experience in dealing with religious questions nor do they have any idea what role in their life's development religion is suppose to play. It's not until we understand why and have experienced the way our parents performed a faith-based act that we realize the pressures that will confront us when we must decide to choose the right way of solving problems. It is not until we have learned how to think and can absorb what we read and hear, without the influences of predetermined opinions, that we are able to reach our own conclusions about anything. In other words, until we are able to think outside the influences of biased opinions and are capable intellectually to challenge previously read or expressed opinions with some degree of knowledgeable opinion, we remain entrapped in this philosophy of bias thinking.

If we have the courage to rely on our faith and believe that Jesus will be there for us, as He is for those who are faithful to His teachings, we will usually perform in an acceptable manner. For example, to have faith that Jesus will help us is like trusting that our actions, in response to a given situation, will result in a morally and ethical behavior and will be acceptable to others and rewarding for us. Faith requires action to be displayed or it does not exist. If we have faith in the Word of God, it is because we believe in the teachings of Jesus who is God-made man. Religious freedom gives us the opportunity to accept or reject what he taught, what he did, and what he foretold, but if we do what is right, we will be blessed with the knowledge to know that our actions will be acceptable to the Lord.

It seems to me, if one believes and studies the Word of God, that a belief in Jesus would be automatic. I have learned over the years that it has been nonacademic interpretations of the Word of God that seem to create more questions than answers for me. I remember when I was in high school, I made conclusions on my own which I thought pretty much summed up both books of the Bible for me. But as I studied and learned, I realized that there had been a lot that I had missed because one has to learn how to understand the Bible as well as read the Bible. In my opinion, however, it seemed obvious that the Old Testament dealt with creation, God's laws, prophecy, and wisdom; and the New Testament began the age of truth with the birth of Jesus. God gave doubters an opportunity to experience His existence and love by giving them Jesus, whom God made in the flesh so that He could be mindful of their ways, thoughts, and reasons for their actions. Being a Jew, His people could better relate to him as a Christian. They could experience His miracles; they could touch Him and hear His words. Anyone who had the opportunity to see and hear Jesus couldn't help knowing that he always displayed endless love. They had to be inspired by his wisdom and passion, touched by his inspiration, and blessed by his miracles.

It is without question that I believe the gospel writers wrote with divine guidance all that they felt compelled to share about the experiences of Jesus in an attempt to hand down what Jesus accomplished, taught, and promised to His people. Whether they wrote under the pen names of Matthew, Mark, Luke, and John or whether they transcribed their thoughts to scribes to be written later is not as important as the value of the lessons that were passed on. We know that there were nonbelievers after having had the opportunity to experience Jesus's life just as there are skeptics in the twentieth century. One could wonder at the beliefs of the scientific genius Albert Einstein who said, "I cannot conceive of a God who rewards and punishes his creatures, or has a will of the kind that we experience in ourselves. Neither can I nor would I want to conceive of an individual that survives his physical death; let feeble souls, from fear or absurd egoism, cherish such thoughts. I am satisfied with the mystery of the eternity of life and with the awareness and a glimpse of the marvelous structure of the existing world, together with the devoted striving to comprehend a portion, be it ever so tiny, of the Reason that manifests itself in nature." **(5)** The following was also written as part of his *New York Times* obituary on April 19, 1955,

"I cannot imagine a God who rewards and punishes the objects of his creation, whose purposes are modeled after our own.—A God, in short, who is but a reflection of human frailty. Neither can I believe that the individual survives the death of his body, although feeble souls harbor such thoughts through fear or ridiculous egotisms." God gave each person on this earth unique personalities, characteristics, and abilities. The sum total of all this is one's ability to make choices. When one examines other major religions of the world, each has specific responsibilities, which are expected to be fulfilled; this is the influence of one God on all humans.

A Student's Summary Interpretation of the New and Old Testaments, Including the Beginning of the Christian Church

The Old Testament Teaches Us
The Stories of Creation
> Includes the birth of the world, man, nature, sin, knowledge, good, and evil

God's Law
> The Ten Commandments

Destruction and New Beginnings of
> Man, cities, countries, and things

The Old Testament Contains Warnings and Prophesies
> The word of the *prophets*
> *The book of Revelation*

Comments on the Book of Revelation:

After reading the book of Revelation and hearing evangelists preaching the doom and gloom of its contents, the end of the world was surely just around the corner. Scholars think it was a sermon to top all sermons, which was meant to shape up the behavior of all who heard it. It appeared to me that Revelation was written by a very mad person who thought the end of the world was near and deserved by the sinners of the world. Its good-versus-evil theme highlighted its portrayal of bad choices and immoral behavior. Only the devil himself could have thought of such a cast of characters as those who filled Revelation. The likes of a seven-headed red dragon with ten horns and wearing crowns, sea beasts roaming the land, and the great whore of Babylon could only be created by a very imaginative writer. "Blessed is he who reads aloud the words of the prophecy, and blessed are those who hear for the time is near." The plot of Revelation foreshadowed in these words is a warning that the end of time and what it will be like is near. The wages of bad choices, the results of greed and jealousy, and the hardships of immoral behavior will be dealt with during the destruction. The story is so corrupted and macaw that the only way the creator of this debauchery—which is the devil himself—can be destroyed is for God himself to whip the slate clean of all who exist and start over. At one point in my studies, I thought the situation, which prompted this sermon, could be likened to the feelings Jesus may have sometimes had as to whether he should go back to Galilee and start over again.

In the year AD 33—Jesus died for our sins, defeating death.

The Divine Revelation
> The beginning of the Christian Church
> The Apostolic and Roman (Location)
> Catholic Church (Universal)

History Taught Me the Facts:

The first Christian emperor of Rome (Constantine brings Christianity to Rome)

The apostles began the Roman (location) Catholic (meaning universal) Church. Peter, who was told by Jesus to build his church, is also credited as being the first Bishop of Rome (the spiritual leader of the Roman Catholic Church).

In AD 380—Christianity became the official religion of the Roman Empire.

During the early years of the church, two statements of faith were developed:
> The Apostles' Creed and the Nicene Creed. These two creeds are said to be the two Christian beliefs that keeps the major braches of Christianity together.

In AD 1054, the east and west parts of the Roman Empire splits into the Eastern Orthodox (Greek) and Roman Catholic religions.

During the sixteenth century, the Protestant Reformation saw the forming of the Protestant denominations.

The Reformation created four main groups:
> Lutherans
> Presbyterians and Congregationalists
> Anglicans
> Anabaptist and Spiritualistic Groups

I always wondered how the different churches got started and where they came from. My studies in biblical history and church history came up with some information:

The Reformation created new Protestant churches:
From the Mennonites came the Amish
Then the Methodist—The Salvation Army for example was founded by a Methodist Preacher in 1865 by the name of William Booth.

From the Lutheran influence came the Calvinists
> *The Baptists*
> *The Presbyterian*
> *The Congregationalists*

Other churches with significant memberships in the 1800s:
> Church of Jesus Christ of Latter-Day Saints
> Jehovah's Witnesses—Charles Russell (1852-1926)
> Christian Scientists—Mary Eddy (1821-1910)
> Unification Church (1954)

From the Anglicans came the Episcopal Church.

MY SUMMARY:
Between the pages of the Old Testament's wisdom and the promises of everlasting life in the New Testament lies our Christian religion and all its mysteries under one God but so many churches.

So Many Churches:

According to David Barrett and team, there are nineteen major world religious groupings in the world, which are subdivided into about 10,000 distinct religions. Of the latter, there were 270 religions and para-religions (independent nonchurch groups like the Fellowship of Christian Athletes), which had over a half-million adherents in the year 2000 CE. Within Christianity, they have identified 34,000 separate groups (denomination, sects, individual unaffiliated churches, parachurch groups, etc.) in the world. **(6)** From *The Age of Faith*, Will Durant writes about religion, "In many aspects religion is the most interesting of man's ways, for it is his ultimate commentary on life and his only defense against death." **(7)**

For Christians, the will of God lights the path to heaven. To help us see the light, he gave us Jesus who taught us how to live our life and what road to follow. It is written that when the spirit, which appeared fifty days after Jesus was crucified, the Christian church was born. The church's traditions began with the work of the twelve disciples. Saint Peter is said to have been the leader chosen by Jesus to lead the Catholic (universal) church. Today, it is not only the biggest church, but also the world's largest organized Christian religion. By the year 380 A.D., it had become the official state religion of the Roman Empire until the Protestant Reformation in the sixteenth century. Today, when we speak about Christians, we have to ask, which ones.

There are three main divisions of the Christian Church: Roman Catholic, Eastern Orthodox (Greek), and Protestant. Bruce Shelley, in his work, *Church History in Plain Language*, said that when the church was "ignited by the resurrection and fueled by the Holy Spirit, the church grew in all directions geographically as well as socially. It was a unified church with a spiritual vision, a conviction that all Christians should be one body, thought of as 'the Holy Catholic Church.'" **(8)** The early church fathers were Catholic not protestant. This is because in the first centuries, the term *Catholic* was widely used by the church in the sense that the church was both universal in contrast to local congregations, and orthodox in contrast to heretical groups. Jesus sent his disciples into the entire world, and Paul had opened the church to the Gentiles. In a sense, Christianity was simply a development of Jesus's plans and Paul's efforts. In the Catholic Encyclopedia, Vol. III, it is suggested that God is the establisher of the perfect religion because there is nothing perfect than Jesus, its founder. His teachers (the apostles) have His spirit, which is the truth ever present.

"Christ established the church in a variety of parables which sketched many of the features of its character and history, all of which point to something external and perceptible by the senses.

> . . . It is the "house built upon a rock" (Matt. 7:24) showing the security and permanence of its foundation, and

> . . . It is "the city set upon a hill" (Matt. 5:14) indicating its visibility.

> . . . Its doctrine works in the three great races descended from Noah's sons like the leaven hidden in three measures of meal, silently, irresistible (Matt. 13:33)

> . . . It grows great from humble beginnings, like the mustard seed (Luke 13:19)

> . . . It is a vineyard, a sheep-fold, and finally a kingdom, all of which images are unintelligible if the bond that unites Christians is merely the invisible bond of charity.

Christianity is a supernatural religion and the only absolute one . . . The Church is not an afterthought, but instituted by God in the fullness of time, and containing a revelation of Himself, which all to whom it has been adequately presented are bound under pain of eternal loss to:

> . . . offer to all, who are sincere in seeking, the solution of all the world's problems;

> . . . enable human nature to raise to the sublimeness heights and "to play the immortal";

> . . . fill itself of mysteries and Divine paradoxes, as bringing the Infinite into contact with the finite;

> . . . live by one bond of civilization, the one condition of progress, the one hope of humanity—love for all who believes.

Not all obey the gospel (Rom. 10:16)
The Jews rejected Christ in spite of the evidence of prophecy and miracle;
The world rejects the Church of Christ, the city set upon a hill, conspicuous though she is through the notes that proclaim her Divine.

What men call the failure of Christianity is no proof that it is not God's final revelation. It only makes evident how real is human liberty and how grave human responsibility. Christianity is furnished with all the necessary evidence to create conviction of its truth, given goodwill.—"He that hath ears to hear, let him hear." **(9)**

Man Made Flesh:

> Christians didn't get it, Jews would not believe it, and society wouldn't live it. God was discouraged, mad, but decided one more chance was due. He thought about it, then said, "Let there be a clear winter's night with a star to guide the way. There will be a manger where the Prince of Peace and love will be born. To defeat death and teach the 'good news' one last time."

WHO SHOULD MAKE THE RULES?

As I matured in age, I never gave much thought anymore about church history but did proceed to develop a philosophical approach to the subject of how we become what we are. It seemed to me that if the mind at birth had no meaningful intelligence and was developed and shaped by its experiences and biased traditions, then it should be reasonable to assume if a society, for example, wanted to have the strongest army, they only needed to control people's experiences toward that end. At this point, it seemed to me that there were two purposes for education: one was to teach people how to do things, and secondly, prepare people to live a life. However, to me, this brought up the problem of individualism. Somebody has to be in control, however, and when individual families make up a society alone then tries to control other's moral behavior and judges what is acceptable and not acceptable in matters of civil and political matters, problems could start to occur.

Everyone knows what morality is but not everyone has the integrity to practice Christian ethics as passed down to us from our Christian heritage. The question then becomes, who determines what the rules are and who enforces them? Certainly, not everyone is going to play by the same rules. Therefore, it seems to me that this dilemma needs to be structured by the lessons learned from our religious and social experiences, supported and tested by our academic education. The philosophy developed as a result, which is considered reasonable and in the best interest of the common good, should be flexible enough to meet future conditions as they change. In most cases, the politics and class structure that occurs determines who is best qualified to enforce the decisions made by society; therefore, it is up to the members of society to determine if those charged with this responsibility practices the moral and ethical standards approved by the majority.

It was Bernard Lonergan who observed that "the ideal basis of society is community, and the community may take its stand on a moral, a religious, or a Christian principle. The moral principle is that men individually are responsible for what they make of themselves, but collectively they are responsible for the world in which they live. Such is the basis of universal dialogue. The religious principle is God's gift of his love, and it forms the basis of a dialogue between all representatives of religion. The Christian principle conjoins the inner gift of God's love with its outer manifestation in Christ Jesus and in those that follow him. Such is the basis of Christian ecumenism." **(10)**

To Learn or Not to Learn: How would we survive without an education? There is so much to learn that we need a procedure to follow, i.e., learn all we can we from the past, by analyzing the results that occurred and by applying safeguards to assure that the same potential for mistakes are protected from decisions that will become obsolete too quickly. By doing this, we can avoid the same mistake or use what worked to create improved results. By this process, we theorize how things could have been done to make the outcome better and are better able to respond with enlightened guesses as to what any given outcome would have been if other considerations had caused other alternatives to be implemented. These processes, when studied and contemplated, can certainly contribute to our ability to make decisions; but are they morally acceptable to the community, in the best interest of the common good, and would God be pleased with the results? As Bertrand Russell pointed out, "If the probable effects are, on the whole better than those of any other action which is possible under the circumstances, then the action is right." **(11)**

Academically, I have always been taught that a searching and critical mind is an essential element in the act of believing. For example, when a new fact caused a change in an important medical belief, it did not cause a disbelief in medicine; likewise, Christians should challenge their understanding of their religious and social beliefs as long as their doubts do not involve a rejection of their belief in God. This is the problem I have with Einstein's observations. One cannot be a Christian and doubt the existence of God for example. As one who had learned most of my prior theology from osmosis and a few college religion courses, I could see my theology maturing when I enrolled in our church-sponsored Pastoral Ministry course of study. I soon found myself taking the position that theological statements, which had no relevance to the life of Christian people even if true, would not be an effective expression of the community's faith and that the biblical statements should be consistent with scientific knowledge and be able to speak to the concerns of contemporary people. In light of this conclusion, I thought it was very important to know what the Bible scholars and church said about various subjects (or at least know where to find it) in order for me to support a position and to develop inspirational thought. Second Timothy 3:16-17, on the subject of learning the truth as written by the divine writers, apparently agreed. Timothy says that scripture "is inspired by God and is useful for teaching for refutation, for correction, and for training in righteousness, so that one who belongs to God may be competent, equipped for every good work."

THE CHURCH INFLUENCES OUR BEHAVIOR:
Religious and cultural backgrounds play a huge role in influencing our behavior. Those who respect their faith, tend to live by its principles and think about what they have been taught before they act. Their plan of action has usually been carefully planned and has included much thought as to the possible effect their decision will have on those involved. Knowing they will live with each decision they make for a long time creates enough incentive for the caring to provide the best answers available. It is, therefore, that which we believe our religious traditions to be that contributes greatly to our reasoning, which in turn

is what motivates our moral actions. Is it fair, is it in the best interest of as many citizens as possible, and will it provide for future expansion? It is only when evil aggression and emotions are allowed to creep into our better judgment that our otherwise acceptable moral behavior is compromised.

Laws and the punishment assigned to breaking those laws create an incentive to avoid what we know to be evil influences, and when making these laws, we need to consider what effect a multicultural tradition and others religious views will become during the enforcement of these laws. In other words, in my mind, leaving God out of the loop or ignoring the faiths of others makes it harder to live by acceptable Christian values and can make the question become, does crime pay or how can I get away with it or what matter will it make to them? On the other hand, is it possible that two and a half million Christians could have gotten it wrong? When we attend church, it is the homilies that remind us how we are suppose to live our life, be faithful believers, and to always try to make our world a better place to live; but "what can we do to make this a better world?" is not a question we ask ourselves enough? We hear in the sermons and homilies every week the call for us to think about the greater good and to strive to achieve a standard of morality that would make God proud, but do we work to do it?

Even Martin Luther, who was trained and educated to live by Christian principles saw a completely different process influencing the religious leaders' life. Roland Herbert Bainton, in his work *The Reformation of the Sixteenth Century*, says, "Nowhere does Martin Luther set forth his views in more rugged and glowing words than in his canticle 'On The Freedom of The Christian Man.'" He quotes Luther as saying, "Faith is produced and preserved in us by preaching why Christ came, what He brought and bestowed, and what benefit it is to us to accept Him." **(12)** But do we live by his principles? "Luther's fundamental break with the Catholic Church," writes Bainton, "was over the nature and destiny of man, and much more over the destiny than the nature." **(13)** Luther's concerns from the 1500s are not so much different from today's concerns, although, Andrew Tevington, a writer of newspaper religious columns says this "faithful living brought order to a chaotic world and morality to a sinful people."

CREATION SCIENCE OR THE BIBLE, WHICH SHOULD IT BE?
Today, the First Amendment of the United States Constitution contains the requirement that there be a separation between church and state. This concept mandates, for example, that our public schools cannot teach any one religion as being better than another nor can they teach that a religious life is better than a worldly life, unbound by monastic restrictions. Since the soul of the Christian religion is centered on the fall of man and original sin, the foreshadowing or need for Jesus as our savior would be counterproductive to the study of the Christian creation story. Liberal Christians, Atheists, and Jews have no problems with the Christian need for a savior because the Jewish interpretations of Genesis dismisses the concept of original sin, and others have concluded that the Christian creation story is just myth.

B. A. Robinson, author of an article appearing on the Web site of the Ontario Consultants on Religious Tolerance writes, "Creation science can be taught in the public schools as part of the regular science curriculum. It can be argued," says Robinson, "that it is important that it be taught in order that the students become fully aware of the range of beliefs about origins. However, in order to be constitutionally correct in the U.S . . . Creation science can only be taught as a concept that some people believe in; it cannot be taught as actual truth, and, . . . Creation science based on the biblical book of Genesis cannot constitutionally be discussed in isolation. The beliefs of other religious and of secular movements would have to be taught along with the Judeo-Christian belief. Otherwise, Judaism and Christianity would be seen as being promoted by the school as superior to other religions and to a secular lifestyle." **(14)**

Does this mean that an opportunity now exists to teach Christianity as part of World history since the discovery of the Dead Sea Scrolls in the middle of the twentieth century have been authenticated? Why not teach Christianity as part of ancient history under the same terms and conditions as science teaches evolution? There may be hope yet. A Texas legislator wants to require the states' 1,700 public school districts to teach the Bible as a textbook, "not a worship document." The bill would mandate that high schools offer history and literature courses on the Old and New Testaments as an elective. In Georgia, two literature classes on the Bible are included on a list of state-approved courses that the public schools could choose to offer beginning next year. The Texas measure would go a step further, requiring districts to make such courses available. Advocates on both sides of the issue agreed. Alabama was the first state to adopt a Bible textbook for high schools. Katherine T. Phan, *Christian Post* reporter in her review of the book says, "The textbook divides the Bible into core themes and shows how each theme or period in the Bible influenced artists, musicians, poets, politicians, and leaders throughout history. It has a particular emphasis on relating the Bible's influence on American figures." The name of the textbook is *The Bible and Its Influence* and is published by the Bible Literacy Project, which is a nonpartisan, nonprofit endeavor to encourage and facilitate the academic study of the Bible in public schools. The organization's Web site is reporting the public school Bible textbook is in 350 Schools and 43 States at the current time. This is indeed a wonderful start.

HOW MANY CHURCHES ARE THERE?

With over 11,000 religions in the world, however, I am not sure how we will ever see a truly meaningful course of religious study that will be influential enough to motivate students in our public schools to adopt much of a Christian attitude. By a Christian attitude, I mean a code of conduct built on the Ten Commandments with integrity originating from a behavior, which reflects the Golden Rule. If the integrity being accepted today is not influenced by the family, students will flock to those churches who feature motivational musicians proclaiming their music in Jesus's name, evangelists who promise everything they want for a love offering, or other houses of worship who are entertaining and feature the most fun things to do, carry a simple message, and suggests what you want you can have. Traditional churches, which some students are attending with their families, are losing out to the mega churches, which offer entertainment in their services.

If better youth programs are not implemented, the interest in going to the traditional churches are likely to be short-lived and the chore of going to worship will become abated by an eventual condescending attitude. The fact is, there have been developed, over the centuries, as many religious theories as there are churches; and I'm not sure it is possible to ever know all there is to know about anyone of them. There have been also many attempts to classify religions in America. Tom W. Smith who produced a paper entitled, "Classifying Protestant Denominations," made one such attempt. While working on his paper, he noticed several

interesting observations, which were made by the reverend J. Gordon
Melton, America's champion church hunter and Edwin S. Gaustad. It was
Melton who said, "We are probably the most religious people and the
most diversely religious people on earth," and Gaustad observed that even
as early as the seventeenth century one found "Huguenots in Charleston,
Anglicans in Tidewater, Virginia, Catholics in St. Mary's City, Swedish
Lutherans alone the Delaware, Dutch Reform in Manhattan, Puritans in
New England, Baptists and heaven knows what else in Rhode Island." **(15)**
Smith goes on to say that, "The French aristocrat, Talleyrand, had observed
as many as thirty-two religions but only one sauce. Since then America has
continued to both import foreign and spawn indigenous religions, until by
the late 1970. Melton came up with a list of 1,187 primary denominations
in the United States and had ignored or treated as separate categories all
remaining denominations. Some classify fundamentalists as one while
others classify fundamentalists into as many as five categories: Orthodox,
Conservative, Neo-Fundamentalists, Evangelical, and Sects." **(16)**

What Smith had done in his report was to develop his own classification
scheme. He breaks down denominations into the associations to which
they belong, i.e., National Council of the Churches of Christ or one of the
three Fundamentalists bodies, the National Evangelical Association, the
Pentecostal Federation of North American, and the Christian Holiness
Association. The next steps were to examine what beliefs they professed,
then examine the qualifications of the clergy, and finally to define the
theological orientation of the denomination. If students are exposed to
the influences the Bible has on people, perhaps they will want to explore
theology on a more academic basis.

CHANGE IS GOOD AND CAN CREATE A LEARNING EXPERIENCE
When I look back at my church experiences, I praise God for the
opportunities I have had to learn about other religions and become
familiar with their member's attitude toward others. My experiences
have involved the Methodist, Lutheran, Episcopalian, Fundamentalist,
and Catholic churches. How is that for a background?

First a Methodist
As a young second grader, my mom would dress me up and point me in
the right direction on the road to the Methodist Church. We walked, in
those days, because there wasn't any public transportation in the country.

Before adult church began, our pastor would tell us a Bible story, always explaining its meaning as he told the story. The pastor was also the choir director. After church, he would have the words for the next Sunday's children's choir hymn written on the back of old wallpaper stretched across several chairs for us to learn. He would read the words, which were printed in black crayon on the blank side of the wallpaper, before having us attempt to sing the hymn. Usually the hymn would require another story to be told, which made the hymn more interesting. I still have a picture of our class and choir in my box of memorabilia. In the summer, the same group of us who sang and made up our Sunday school class enjoyed lots of activities and fun at vacation Bible school. Those were fun days. The most important thing I learned would live with me forever: "Jesus loves me."

DAD WAS AN EPISCOPALIAN:

I was almost a teenager when my dad made us an offer, and that was, if we would all go to the Episcopal Church, he would take us to the city for services. Dad was an orphan at the age of five and was raised by his sisters who faithfully attended the local Episcopal Church; it was easy to understand his loyalty. Since he had the only driver's license in the family, it was either continue to walk to the Methodist Church to attend Sunday school and church with my friends or ride fifteen miles away to go to the Episcopal church with my family. My mother (devoted Methodist) explained how important it was for us to attend church together as a family, and since dad was willing to go with us, we should enjoy the experience together. For the first time, we all went to church together.

Rev. Pateman was a tall lanky man at 6'1". He had played center on the University of Virginia's basketball team, which impressed me then, but today, he probably wouldn't have been a point guard given the height players are these days. He was a wonderful, warm-hearted man who was very much like a mother hen to his flock. He soon had me reading the New Testament lessons on Sunday morning and, in the Episcopal tradition, decked me out in a white blouse, draped over a black robe, carrying the crucifix on a tall poll during the opening procession. All of this was quite different from my days at the Richmond Methodist Church. When I became sixteen, I was confirmed and became a full-fledged Episcopalian. Dad's love for his church had brought our family together in religious thought.

A DIFFERENT POINT OF VIEW:

At eighteen, I started college and experienced, for the first time in my life, the lessons of the Bible and the teachings of Jesus from an academic point of view. I found it fascinating to discuss theological and philosophical subjects in class and then later with friends over coffee. Until this time, I had never thought about the Bible stories we read or the teachings of Jesus from any other perspective than what the story was about. I had never worried or thought about why these stories were written, for whom they were written, or for what purpose they were written. Now, and maybe it was because I was older and more interested, these questions were important and the stories more interesting to talk about.

This experience was giving me more reasons for going to church, and going to church seemed to be making more sense; I was learning the truth, which made the relationship between my life and the Bible stories exciting. Understanding Jesus's teachings seemed to help develop a bond between my religious beliefs and me. The church's explanation on matters such as rituals, moral issues, and social correctness made more sense when scripture substantiated them. When I understood that the church's teachings were a result of years of study involving the original documents, archeological findings, and other historical data, a whole new world opened up for me to think about. I learned how women was created from a man's rib, the origin of the institution of marriage, all about Abraham, Isaac, and Jacob—our patriarchs—sin and death through Adam, the symbol of the church in Noah's Ark, the symbolism of water, the importance of baptism, the foreshadowing of Christ's sacrifice in the story of Abraham's willingness to sacrifice his son, and all this in the first book of the Old Testament, Genesis.

THE LUTHERAN EXPERIENCE:

Because I did not have the means to attend college continually, I had to stop from time to time to go to work until I could afford to continue. As I anticipated, Uncle Sam caught up with me and invited me to spend some time with him in his army. After basic training, I was assigned a position at the U.S. army headquarters in Heidelberg, Germany. A year later, I was transferred to the Southern Area Command Headquarters in Munich where I stayed until discharged. There are basically two major faiths in Germany: Lutheran in the North and Catholic in the South.

After a year in Munich, I met and eventually married a German girl from a little town in North East Bavaria. Interestingly, I was the first American to ever be married in this small-town Evangelical Lutheran Church. In Germany, the mayor must marry you, which is the legally recognized procedure. If desired, the church will also perform marriage vows. When my service obligation ended, we went back to Ohio, and I applied for financial help utilizing the GI Bill. With this financial help, I was able to complete the final requirements needed to earn my teaching degree. As it turned out, my first teaching job also included coaching football and tennis. One of my football-coaching colleagues was a lifelong member of the American Lutheran Church and invited us to join his family for Sunday services, which we did.

OPPORTUNITY KNOCKS:
Like most teachers, I found it necessary to work a second job. During that first summer, I studied and passed the test required to be a licensed insurance agent. I continued to work part-time during the school year and was full-time in the summer. With the increased income, we decided to buy a house and moved out of the area. Not long after we had moved, I met a Lutheran minister who was the pastor of a Missouri Synod Lutheran Church near our new neighborhood. I was not sure what the difference in Lutheran Churches was, but we accepted his invitation to come to his church. Within a few months, I was nominated to be considered for church council. By the casting of lots, I was elected. As I grew in the insurance business, I started to think about quitting my teaching job in exchange for a full-time career in the insurance business. The opportunity to do this occurred several months later but involved a move to another state. After careful thought, we decided that I should stop teaching and move to Louisiana to build a career in the insurance business.

BACK TO THE METHODIST:
We settled in a small community in Southwest Louisiana known as Cajun country. It was called that because of its historical French Canadian connection. The only disadvantage to this small community was our church choices. When it was time to attend church, we could drive a hundred miles, to a larger town, to attend a Lutheran or Episcopal church; or we could go to the Baptist, Methodist, or the Catholic Church were we lived. Since we had three children by this time and wanted them to

participate in Sunday school, vacation Bible school, and family church activities, we selected the Methodist Church. My church life had gone full circle it seemed; I was now back where I had started as a youngster, with the Methodist Church. First Methodist, then Episcopalian, next Lutheran, and now back to Methodist. The next few years were filled with many interesting experiences, which I shall not forget. Although the experiences and friends we met in this small Cajun community were unique, we felt the benefits of living in a larger community would be better for all of us. After several years in Cajun country, we decided to move to the larger city of Baton Rouge.

BACK TO THE LUTHERAN:

I could have never guessed that this move was going to present me with yet another unique religious opportunity. Not long after we had set up housekeeping and was becoming settled, a Sunday afternoon knock at the door became an opportunity to be part of a pastor's challenge. Introducing himself was an American Lutheran pastor who told us that he had been commissioned by his bishop to build a new church in our neighborhood. He explained that if we were interested he would tell us all about it. When he found out that my wife was a lifelong Lutheran and all three kids were baptized Lutheran, he was elated. We agreed to help him build a new church. With that decision, another new experience began. In the beginning, we would meet at the pastor's home, but it was not long until we had bought a large parcel of land nearby and was converting the existing buildings into a church. I became the first treasurer and was asked to build the church's first altar for Sunday services, which I did. By now, it seemed I had gone full turn several times. What was God saying to me, "Go back and get it right?" or was he saying, "Learn all you can learn before making a final decision." I was brought up Methodist but became an Episcopalian. I got married and became Lutheran and even served on the church council. A move caused us to go back to the Methodist, and now I was helping to build a new Lutheran Church. What a ride!

FAITH NEVER FAILS:

Though the next several years of my life were not very pleasant, it was the lessons I had learned from my past church experiences that brought me through the heartaches that I was about to experience. I remember when I first realized that I was going to experience a completely new world. It was around midnight, somewhere in Texas, there weren't any cars on the road anymore and the stores of the little town I had just driven through had long been closed. As I drove pass the feed mill, on the edge of town, I could see the streetlights through my rearview mirror, shining faithfully as if they were in charge of guarding the town and all its treasures. Soon it got black again, and I realized for the first time, I have no place to go!

Everything I owned was in the car I was driving—sooner or later, I thought, they'll probably take that too, then what will I do? As I reflected over the last several months, I tried to find a reason for what went wrong. I kept asking myself the age-old question, why is this happening to me? Later that evening, as I drove through one small town after another not knowing where I was going to end up, I remembered a line from John Steinbeck's *The Grapes of Wrath*, which later in my life became a phrase with special meaning, "If you're having trouble or hurt or need help go to poor people. They're the only ones that'll help." **(17)** I didn't know it then but later realized that the meaning and reality of that line and what was happening to me now would change my attitude in the future about those who were experiencing social difficulties.

Although I have never had to sleep in cardboard boxes, I have known others including children who were spending long restless evenings sleeping in less than acceptable conditions. Time after time, I found myself waking up sad because decent people were trying to exist in terrible conditions with all their possessions crammed into shopping bags. The world of the homeless was very far from mine—but in some ways, it was quite near. The depression I felt, the challenges of overcoming rejection, homelessness, and the lost of my self-worth were eventually overcome by my faith that Jesus would help me through this terrible time in my life. For any of us, the loss of a job, the death of a spouse or a child, a severe physical disability, or family problems could be the next thing we experience. Total despair could be on its way to you or someone you know. For many homeless people, their tragedies were not foreseen, they were unexpected events that caused them to experience a major life experience. Regardless of the cause, tragedies happen. Whether they are caused by nature, illness, loss of a job, or being struck by a personal tragedy that makes you feel less than human is not pleasant.

The people who seek shelter in thousands of cities across America because they have no home have been deserted by their families and friends they once had and are now forced to survive however they are able. Like any other problem, we can choose whether we will allow ourselves to be defeated by this experience or emerge stronger for seeking solutions and help from others. Being homeless was not in my master plan. And although it was not a very pleasant experience, I never had to do anything illegal to survive. This is the time we ask, "What can I do?" and tap our hidden resources and strengths. This is the time we are forced to turn to others for help, such as our community agencies, to religion for strength and guidance. If you have never witnessed the despair of the homeless firsthand, it is easier to ignore them. That is what I was seeing. It seemed that people assumed that homeless people were all derelicts, mentally ill, drug addicts—people beyond help, people who don't deserve assistance.

I was glad that I had learned that faith was the central requirement for believers. I reflected on the story of Job and thought about how his faith brought him through all the hardships he had to endure. I remembered my religion professor saying that it was the poor that followed and accepted Jesus the most and what my dad had said to me the first time I went out by myself as a teenager, "I can't always be with you wherever you go," he said, "but I have faith that you'll do what's right." My dad's anticipation was that my behavior would reflect an action that would be morally correct. The manner in which I acted (my behavior) was the anticipated response to the situation I would find myself in. What my dad had faith in was that I would make a decision, which would be right in the eyes of God. It was going to be my faith in God that would help me be safe and make decisions that would reflect that faith. Faith to me was the act performed in response to my belief. I had skills, I was able to think, and I knew the difference between right and wrong. Now was certainly not the time to turn my back on everything I knew was right. Think about what you would do in such a situation then make a plan to handle it. Is it easy to do?

GOD DOES HAVE A PLAN FOR US: The next year found me with a new wife and a new work experience in a new part of the country. From the first week we started to date, we went to church on Sunday, alternating between her Catholic Church and my Episcopal Church.

Eventually I realized that I wanted to share the communion experience with her and my new family but unless one of us made a conversion decision that was not going to happen.

Little did I know that I would be challenged again to make a major religious change in my life; but this time, it would be one that would make me feel closer to God and more thankful for the life of Jesus and his blessings. The question was, did I want to make the commitment to leave my Episcopal Church to join the Catholic Church? I knew these two churches had been one church before Henry VIII and that the liturgy and theology was akin to one another, but even though I had learned most of my Christian values by osmosis and not by any real religious scholarly training, I felt I would be more happy in the church I was raised. I felt like I was well prepared to meet my maker if he desired to meet me. I had learned the importance of integrity and the value of faith, hope, charity; and I knew how to live by the Christian principles of morality. Additionally, I knew that the church I had belonged to for the past forty-plus years would continue to take care of my religious needs. I considered my church the house that Jesus built, the church of my father and mother, the one in which I had been baptized and confirmed, and the one where I celebrated communion. What else did I need?

In the final analysis, I knew God loved me, what he expected of me, and that he died for my sins so that I could experience everlasting life. It didn't matter to me what I was called. The truth is, I would have never considered leaving my church had I not loved my Catholic wife so much and wanted to share in the full communion experience with her. Her faith was like a rock, and I was intrigued by this religion that made her so loyal and its members so faithful.

The Role of the Church and Our Relationship to It:
In the traditional view of Jesus, a unique incarnation of the spirit of God made him man. To Christians, Jesus was the only human who avoided the temptations of sin to the extent that he was in perfect union with God. Christ showed that salvation from the stagnation and evils of sin was possible. By the grace of God, and because we regard him as our personal savior and the redeemer of all, He is always with us in spirit. In this sense then, Christ is a sacrament. It is possible, therefore, that those who accept Christ as their savior and live as he did become sacraments

to others. And since the church is a source of salvation and because, through the community, people are introduced to Christ and to the life he made possible in the church, the church can therefore be considered to be a sacrament—a sign of Christ and a source of God's grace. It is the sacrament that challenges us to live the life Jesus lived. When people love something or someone, it is very natural to want to share all things together, so it is with the Christian family. The church is neither a building nor an organization; it is a community of people who are joined together through baptism. The people forming this community believe that Jesus Christ is both God and man, that he came upon this earth suffered, died, and was raised from the dead to glory. This community comes together in the one Christ, shares each other's joys, and experiences each other's sorrows. This community, which knows that Christ is God and responds fully to this knowledge, is called the Christian community in the church.

St. Paul used the image of the "body of Christ" to speak about the community of the New Testament. In First Corinthians 12:12-14, "For just as the body is one and has many members, and all the members of the body, though many, are one body, so it is with Christ. Foe in the one Spirit we were all baptized into one body—Jew or Greeks, slaves or free—and we were all made to drink of one Spirit. Indeed the body does not consist of one member but of many." St. Paul emphasizes that we, the church, need one another to truly make Christ present here on earth. The community of the Church, then, is joined to Christ in such a way that Christ and the community become one with each other. Christ brings redemption to the community and we, by entering the community, share in this redemption. Just as a candidate seeking entrance into the community of the Church prepares properly for his or her spiritual journey into the community, the community is urged to renew its commitment in faith and love to Christ and his gospel. Entering into the life of another or others is not for the faint of heart. The demands are great, as are the rewards.

This is the life to which we are called as Christians, and it rests with the church community of persons whose faith experience centers on Jesus of Nazareth to understand and interpret the faith experience of the community. Because of this responsibility, it becomes very important for everyone going through adult Christian formation to understand the history of the church as is developed in the Acts of the Apostles. Acts describes how the church began, who Christians are, and what they are meant to do. As the life of the church continued beyond the period of its origins, however, its members became more and more numerous. And as those members took on the task of living the meaning and message of Jesus in diverse cultures in different parts of the world, the relationship of the Christian people to God came to be expressed in ways less and less similar to the religious practices of earlier times. So that this doesn't happen again and to protect the liturgy approved, for example in the Roman Catholic Church, Pope John II wrote that any liturgy that is not in agreement with the church is considered a falsification. Therefore, in the tradition of the church, it is very important that liturgy be studied and understood not only in its immediate theological and practical features, but also in its broader theological spiritual, historical, aesthetic, social, scientific, and pastoral dimensions. The liturgy, which describes the work of the people in which God is praised and glorified, should be a critical part of one's educational experience coming into the church.

After much prayer, I made the decision to enter what the church called the Journey of Faith program. This program was an opportunity for persons considering joining the Catholic faith to find out more about the church and its traditions. Besides wanting to share in the Eucharistic experience with my wife and family, I wanted to experience a greater intimacy with Jesus Christ, which was of paramount importance to me. With God's grace, the sincerity of the educational staff, the clergy, and the encouragement of my wife sponsor, I completed the nine months of study feeling that I had made the right choice. The rewards of my successful faith journey included a positive religious experience and an entirely new faith community to help support me on my religious and educational journey. I experienced a complete marriage encounter that I knew would bond our life together as husband and wife. Most importantly, feeling the presence of Jesus during the Eucharist and being able to share this with my family brought a new and deeper understanding to the term *life with God* for me.

Shortly after my confirmation, I enrolled in a program conducted by Newman University in Wichita, Kansas, and sponsored by the Oklahoma Dioceses called the Pastoral Ministry Program. This was an opportunity to earn a bachelor of arts degree in pastoral ministry by taking thirty

hours of concentrated theology courses and adding these hours to
the degree work already earned. No other church denomination had
a relationship with a university to offer college theology courses like
these for its people. This program was not just for Catholics, we had an
Episcopal deacon who took classes with us as well as members of other
denominations. Some of them were involved in prison ministry while
others wanted the education in order to be a better Stephen Minister,
for example, or to work in many of the area's Christian schools and
hospitals. I knew it had to be God's love and guidance that directed
me to this program. After completing the required study, I felt more
knowledgeable and religiously confident about my beliefs.

Knowing more about how God's love is manifested, learning about the
Paschal Mystery, being exposed to the wisdom of church documents,
exploring the true meaning and principles behind the sacraments,
reflecting on the principles of what constitutes a Christian life, and
discussing a scholarly interpretation of scriptures were just a few things
the program exposed me to which greatly influenced my religious life.
On the evening of my confirmation, I couldn't help reflect over my
Christian life's experiences; I felt proud that I had found the courage
to begin a new religious journey blessed by the church. I was about to
begin a new religious life with my two new brides: my wife and church.
None of us ever knows what the future will hold. God does have a plan
for us, but most of the time, he just doesn't share it with us until we are
capable of successfully completing the responsibilities they carry with
them.

The Willingness to Change Helps Us to Make Better Life Choices:
Faith teaches us that *change* is not always a bad word; it's what happens in
life. In fact, I think it's our openness to change, to the ongoing invitation
of the spirit that may well be the gift of God we need most. I feel it
was God's grace that was responsible for my conversion to the Catholic
faith and what eventually led me to enroll in the Pastoral Ministry
Program at Newman University. I felt like I was being challenged to
be a better Catholic Christian. Now if I can somehow influence others
to develop those ethical principles, which will encourage them to be
morally responsible and to choose the common good when the demands
of society conflict with their personal desires, then I will feel that I have

made, not only a contribution to their religious life, but that they will also make a positive contribution to society.

HOW DO WE MAKE RELIGIOUS CHOICES?

In my view, it is our family history, experiences, and traditions that usually make us members of a particular church or faith regardless of what it is called. Some others may feel the need to join a church after many years of being a nonbeliever or perhaps they have experienced God's grace in a personal way and want to become part of the church. People change for various reasons, and people become interested in belonging to a church for various reasons. For example, Episcopalians become Catholic because the Catholic Church's liturgy may seem to be too formal. Some Catholics have become Lutheran because they feel that the hierarchy of the Lutheran church is less strict in their interpretation of church theology. Others change because a close friend, future spouse, or pastor has inspired them to share their religion with them, and others change because their church leaders have made theological decisions which the members do not agree is within the church's tradition. Educational experiences often make a difference; for example, when there has been a serious, in-depth study and interest in the Bible, what has been learned may create a desire to want to explore a different religious experience more in tune with the newly learned thoughts on the subject.

I find it personally interesting that there are those who have taken the time to formerly study different theologies but refuse to be a part of a church community. Others may be influenced by a particular pastor with no denominational connections, but because he preaches a good sermon and provides good entertainment at their services, they want to belong. I think one should be obligated to learn as much as possible about his or her particular faith and church's beliefs. The faithful do not need to fear that an attitude of disbelief will develop because they ask questions or discuss, with curiosity and doubt, the reliability of their church's position on a particular subject or practice. Unless their faith was very weak in the first place, they need not fear that academic or formal study will cause them to lose respect for their faith's beliefs. The practice of asking questions about their church's theology and discussing new ideas are ways to strengthen one's faith not lose it. When the Dead Sea Scrolls were found, for example, in the twentieth century, did anyone's beliefs change or had it been strengthened?

Some denominations who resort to calling other faiths disrespectful names such as cults, mackerel snappers, or holy rollers should take note that believing in church theology, regardless of the denomination, doesn't make one a loyal fanatic, social behavior does. The difference is we ask questions in order to grow, which is an important step in the learning curve. While most Christians share the same beliefs, there is much debate on such things as the inerrancy of the Bible, the born-again experience, and the existence of hell, to name a few. There are some wonderful moral people who are nonbelievers in the trinity, the virgin birth, the inerrancy of the Bible, etc. On the other hand, one could spend a lifetime studying the ancient scriptures, history, and archeology only to find that opinions are different from scholar to scholar. Different translations of holy scriptures lead denominations to have different interpretations. This does not mean they believe that the holy scriptures were not divinely written, it means that in the process of translations from Hebrew to Arabic to Greek to English, some words may have been misinterpreted somewhere along the way. Without dedicated Biblical scholars to guide us, there are many thoughts and stories, which can be read by ten different people that will produce ten different interpretations. The voice of Jesus tells us, "Ask and it will be given to you; seek and you will find; knock and the door will be opened to you." For everyone who asks, receives; and the one who seeks, finds; and to the one who knocks, the door will be opened. Hear what Jesus says, "Which one of you would hand his son a stone when he asks for a loaf of bread or a snake when he asks for a fish? If you then, who are wicked, know how to give good gifts to your children, how much more will your heavenly Father give good things to those who ask him" (Matt. 7:7-11). This seems to me, to be Jesus's way of saying that I should seek out the truth by asking questions, even St. Augustine urged Christians to be always reforming the church.

"Words are a human invention," explains Father Kenneth G. Morman of the Diocese of Toledo, Ohio, "which are bound to a particular period of history, changing nuance and even meaning over time and most serious of all they are born of human experiences . . . . They are inspired human words, and therefore have all the limitations intrinsic to human words. In the study of the Scriptures, one must be careful not to substitute our own wisdom for the Lord's deciding in advance how we want God to have proceeded and then staunchly refusing to consider any other possibility."

(18) "Words," adds Dr. Laura, "have a tremendous potential impact upon situations and people—they can convey compassion and encouragement, blessing, and love. Or they can kill spirits and relationships." **(19)** Rev. Morman assures his students that modern mainline academic scripture scholarship in no way weakens our deeply held belief that the scriptures are "wholly and entirely, with all their parts, the true word of God." **(20)** We are reminded in Isaiah 55:10, "For just as from the heavens the rain and snow come down and do not return there till they have watered the earth, making it fertile and fruitful, so shall my word be that goes forth from my mouth—it shall not return to me void, but shall do my will achieving the end for which I sent it."

IN THE EARLY DAYS OF AMERICA:

There were in the past, those that took exception to Christian theology but always emphasized the importance of maintaining an ethical behavior in all their endeavors and were promoters of social justices. Some of them attended Harvard, William and Mary, and the College of New Jersey, which is now called Princeton; and they always maintained a profile that reflected a strong and ethical character. They were called Founding Fathers. Among the most notable included George Washington, Thomas Jefferson, James Madison, Benjamin Franklin, John Adams, and James Monroe. These men respected the idea of God; they understood the universe to be governed by moral and religious forces and prayed for divine protection against the enemies of this world, wrote Jon Meacham in his work *American Gospel*. One thing is for certain, they did not want to establish another government that would be unduly influenced by the church as it was in Britain, but one that would keep Christian characteristics as its guiding light while making decisions.

David Holmes, in his work, *The Faiths of the Founding Fathers*, writes that General George Washington was never confirmed and avoided the sacrament of Holy Communion and that the general was more concerned with morality and ethics than with adhering to the doctrines of any one particular church. He seemed to have no interest in theology. **(21)** However, Meacham writes, "While Washington appears to have thought religion a useful tool in leading his troops and, later his nation, Washington believed that every man was accountable to God alone for his religious opinions and ought to be protected in worshipping the Deity according to the dictates of his own conscience." **(22)** We only need to look at Thomas

Jefferson as a perfect example of this philosophy who wrote his own version of the New Testament called *The Life and Morals of Jesus*. His version of the New Testament was not published, however, until after his death in 1826. Jon Meacham in *American Gospel* says, Jefferson, for one, relished theology, but saw theological debates as private intellectual affairs not fit subjects for government. He said, "I write with freedom, because while I claim a right to believe in one God, I yield freely to others that of believing in three. Both religions I find, make honest men, and that is the only point society has any right to look to." **(23)**

John Adams was the first president who was a Unitarian, which according to Holmes "was a form of super-naturalist Christianity that taught that God was one—unit—and not three-a tri-unit." In doing so, says Holmes, "Unitarian's asserted that they had restored the original Christian belief that Jesus was in some way Commissioned or sent by God but that he remained subordinate to him. Adam's believed the world should follow ethical teachings of Jesus and viewed himself as a Christian." **(24)** But Meacham observed that "the God of the Declaration is a divine force that created the universe, endow all men with human rights, and is an actor in the drama of the world he made." He goes on to say that the founders "made the choice to link the cause of liberty to the idea of God while at the same time avoid sectarian religious imagery or associations." **(25)**

It seems to me, religion compliments government. The character of the founders was very much influenced by Christian morals and ethical behavior, the two ingredients required to be a person of good character. If a government is to succeed in a global world, it is necessary for its decision makers to be men and women who maintain the monumental task of keeping morality, ethics, and the principles of respect for all in their attempt of fulfilling their goals. The founders knew, for example, that America was a pluralistic nation made up of citizens with many faiths and cultures who had to live together. "Franklin, Jefferson, and Adams," writes Meacham, "suggested *E. Pluribus Unum*—'Out of many, one' as the first of the country's three mottoes, these words underscore the pluralistic nature of the American experiment. In addition, God did not disappear entirely. The 'Eye of Providence' contains the second motto, *Annuit Coeptis*—'God has favored our undertakings.' In addition, the third motto, *Novus Ordo Seclorum*, 'a new order of the ages.'" **(26)**

Religion to these founders was "based more on a religion of reason than of revelation," **(27)** wrote Meacham! Their consensus, however, saw religion and moral conduct bound together. History cannot examine the heart of any man's soul for the purposes of judging his religious beliefs, but history can paint a picture of a man's greatness by observing his behavior, morals, and ethical practices. It seems, for these six founders—Franklin, Washington, Adams, Jefferson, Madison and Monroe—even though they did not all view religion in the same "theological" content, they embraced Deism because it excluded the emotional and mysterious aspects of religion, while at the same time, they all lived and reflected an ethical behavior, concludes Holmes. All but Franklin, who according to Holmes, . . . came to believe that religious toleration was vital to a free society. He believed that humans served God best when they performed good works on behalf of humanity and society." **(28)** Holmes quotes Franklin as having once defined a good Christian as "someone who is a good parent, a good child, a good husband or wife, a good neighbor or friend, and a good citizen." **(29)** "The Founders continued to worship, at least occasionally in the church of their ancestors—and their wives and daughters were usually devout supporters of it . . . The impress of their religious background remained strong, even though their questioning of certain of their church's fundamental doctrines led them to Deism," **(30)** says Holmes. The founders knew that no one theology could be mentioned in their new country's documents, but they did recognize the importance of emphasizing the citizens' need to maintain respect for the principles of their own personal theology. They stressed a respect for life, God, country, nature, and the need to maintain a lifestyle that would reflect acceptable moral and ethical standards of behavior while living under the laws of our nation. Holmes quotes a response made by Franklin five weeks before his death in regard to an inquiry from a Congregationalist minister who was president of Yale College, Franklin replied, "Here is my Creed: I believe in one God, Creator of the Universe: That He governs the world by his Providence. That he ought to be worshipped. That the most acceptable service we can render to him is doing good to his other children. That the Soul of man is immortal, and will be treated with justice in another life, respecting its con duct in this. These I take to be the fundamental principles of all sound religion." **(31)**

THE GLUE THAT KEEPS IT TOGETHER; FUNDAMENTALIST BELIEVE LITERALLY

For me, growing up in an atmosphere where the Bible was taken so literally, created more questions than answers. In the overall scheme of things, this type of fundamentalist approach seemed to create a no-win situation for the truth. What I was experiencing was one person's interpretation of a Bible story, decorated with his/her self-serving quotations, the next speaker then countered with a different interpretation of the same story with other selected supporting biblical quotations. I just knew there had to be a better way to learn the truth about the Bible and to experience the real meaning of the lessons it was trying to teach. To me, the central fact that God revealed himself to man through Jesus Christ, even though it may be accepted or rejected, becomes as the act of God not a matter for debate but the supreme event in history. In an article I read during my studies entitled, "How to Understand the Bible," I realized that the basic beliefs that I had developed over the years, although religiously sound, were founded on a strong faith in God and not because of any real academic knowledge. I had to agree with St. Jerome, when he said, "Farming, building, carpentry, etc., all require an apprenticeship, but when it comes to interpreting God's word any doddering old fool can blithely dissect and have a go at explaining it." Although I do not consider myself to be a doddering old fool, I do understand the point being made.

When you consider the sources for obtaining biblical guidance which I was exposed to with the sources used by the biblical scholar, it is obvious that more doubt and questions are raised by using the Fundamentalist approach than that of the historical-critical methods. For example, the historical-critical approach uses techniques first used as far back as the seventeenth century French priest Richard Simon. In his three-volume work entitled, *A Critical History of the Old Testament*, Simon uses techniques that have come to be known as the modern approach to the study of the Bible. "This method takes advantage of historical research, literary analysis, and the finding of archaeology, anthropology, and other sciences. It is historical in as much as scholars seek to discover the social, economic, political, and cultural setting of the times and critical, in that experts judge and evaluate the text and its narrative in the light of literary analysis and scientific information." The biblical scholar's lack of errors is due therefore in part to his dedication to accuracy in utilizing all the sources available. Because of the biblical scholar's work, I have learned that the Bible is really, "God's word in human terms" and that the New Testament is more than just the gospels and other writings, it is a "promise" that when man makes the decision to freely commit himself to God, then he will possess the ultimate faith and will experience the ultimate love of God.

THOU SHALT VERSUS THOU MAYEST: In John Steinbeck's wonderful novel *East of Eden*, Adam Trask, whom Steinbeck uses to parallel the Adam in Genesis, is having a conversation with Lee, his Chinese houseman, and Samuel Hamilton, Adam's friend, about the Cain and Abel story. It is a wonderful example of how, without the biblical scholars' help we can reach conclusions based on our own feelings, common sense skills, the persuasion of others, or just plain talking about it. Lee points out to the group that he is troubled by the different interpretations one can find from two different Bible translations of the same story. Lee tells Samuel when he read Genesis 4:1-16 how it bit deeply into me and I went into it word for word. The more I thought about the story, the more profound it became to me. Then I compared the translations we have—and they were fairly close. There was only one place that bothered me. The King James Version says this—it is when Jehovah has asked Cain why he is angry. Jehovah says, 'If thou doest well, shalt thou not be accepted? And if thou doest not well, sin lieth at the door. And into thee shall be his desire, and thou shalt rule over him.' It was the thou shalt that struck me, because it was a promise that Cain would conquer sin.

Samuel nodded. And his children didn't do it entirely, he said.

Lee sipped his coffee.

Then I got a copy of the American Standard Bible. It was very new then, and it was different in this passage. It says, 'Do thou rule over him.' Now this is very different. This is not a promise, it is an order. And I began to stew about it. I wondered what the original word of the original writer had been that these very different translations could be made." **(33)**

Lee goes on to tell Adam and Samuel that he and his Chinese family who were deep thinkers could study Hebrew and come up with the answer—they even hired a rabbi who was very learned. After two years of intense studying together, they felt "'that we could approach your sixteen verses of the fourth chapter of Genesis,' Lee said. The old gentlemen felt the words, 'Thou Shalt' and 'Do Thou' were very important. And this was the gold from our mining: 'Thou Mayest.' Thou Mayest rule over sin. 'Don't you see?' Lee cried. 'The American Standard translation orders man to triumph over sin, and you can call sin ignorance. The King James translation makes a promise in "Thou Shalt." Meaning that men will surely triumph over sin. But the Hebrew word, the word Timshel—"Thou Mayest"—that gives a choice. It might be the most important word in the world. That says the way is open. That throws it right back on a man. For if "Thou Mayest"—it is also true that "Thou Mayest not."'"

Samuel said, 'I see. But you do not believe this is divine law. Why do you feel its importance?'

"There are many millions in their sects and churches who feel the order, 'Do Thou,' and throw their weight into obedience. And there are millions more who feel predestination in 'Thou Shalt,' Nothing they may do can interfere with what will be. But 'Thou Mayest'! Why, that makes a man great, that gives him stature with the gods, for in his weakness and his filth and his murder of his brother he has still the great choice."

"Lee and his elders have come to the conclusion, 'So we have in the King James version it says . . .' and thou shalt rule over him" which can be interpreted as a promise; The New American says, . . . "you can be his master," which can be taken to mean, you can if you make the right choice. Or we have in the American Standard edition, "Do thou rule over him" which is not a promise, not a matter of choice but seems to be an order. Then there is the Jewish term, "Timshel" which means, "Thou Mayest." It is the conclusion of the group that it is "Thou Mayest"! Why, that makes a man great, that gives him stature with the gods, for in his weakness and his filth and his murder of his brother he has still the great choice."' **(34)**

Steinbeck is saying despite the fact that Adam and Eve have made all humans imperfect, sinful beings, the idea that evil can be overcome by making morality a free choice has been established. He says, "And this I believe: that the free exploring mind of the individual human is the most valuable thing in the world. And this I would fight for; the freedom of the mind to take any direction it wishes, undirected," and so it is today, we do have choices and God does guarantee evil is one of them.

In another scene, Adam, Samuel, and Mr. Lee are trying to name Adam's twins.

"'Two stories have haunted us and followed us from our beginning,' Samuel said, 'We carry them along with us like invisible tails—the story of original sin and the story of Cain and Abel. In addition, I do not understand either of them. I do not understand them at all but I feel them. Lisa gets angry with me. She says I should not try to understand them. She says why we should try to explain a verity. Maybe she's right—maybe she's right.'

"'Lee, Liza says you're a Presbyterian—do you understand the Garden of Eden and Cain and Abel?'

"'She thought I should be something, and I went to Sunday school long ago in San Francisco. People like you to be something, preferably what they are.'

"Adam said, 'He asked you if you understood.'

"'I think I understand the fall. I could perhaps feel that in myself. However, the brother murder—no. Well maybe I don't remember the details very well.'

"Samuel said, 'Most people don't read the details. The details astonish me. And Abel had no children.' He looked up at the sky, 'Lord, how the day passes! It is like a life—so quickly when we do not watch it and so slowly when we do. No,' he said, 'I'm having enjoyment. And I made a promise to myself that I would not consider enjoyment a sin. I take a pleasure in inquiring into things. I have never been content to pass a stone without looking under it. And it is a black disappointment to me that I can never see the far side of the moon.'"

What follows is a group discussion of the meaning God had in mind for telling the story of Cain and Abel and who is to blame for sin. Adam says, "I remember being a little outrage at God. Both Cain and Abel gave what they had, and God accepted Abel and rejected Cain. I never thought that was a just thing. I never understood it. Do you?"

"'Maybe we think out of a different background,' said Lee. 'I remember that this story was written by and for a shepherd people. They were not farmers. Wouldn't the god of shepherds find a fat lamb more valuable than a sheaf of barley? A sacrifice must be the best and most valuable.'

"'Yes, I can see that,' Samuel said. 'And Lee, let me caution you about bringing your Oriental reasoning to Liza's attention.'

"Adam was excited, 'Yes, but why did God condemn Cain? That's an injustice.'

"Samuel said, 'There's an advantage to listening to the words. God did not condemn Cain at all. Even God can have a preference, can't he? Let's suppose God liked lamb better than vegetables. I think I do myself. Cain brought him a bunch of carrots maybe, And God said, "I don't like this. Try again. Bring me something I like and I'll set you up alongside your brother." However, Cain got mad. His feelings were hurt. And when a man's feelings are hurt he wants to strike at something, and Abel was in the way of his anger.'

"After continued discussion, Lee says to Samuel, 'I think this is the best-known story in the world because it is everybody's story. I think it is the symbol story of the human soul . . . . The greatest terror a child can have is that he is not loved and rejection is the hell he fears. I think everyone in the world to a large or small extent has felt rejection. In addition, with rejection comes anger, and with anger some kind of crime in revenge for the rejection, and with the crime guilt—and there is the story of humankind. I think that if rejection could be amputated, the human would not be what he is. Maybe there would be fewer crazy people. I am sure in myself there would not be many jails. It is all there—the start, the beginning. One child, refused the love he craves, kicks the cat and hides his secret guilt; and another steals so that money will make him loved; and a third conquers the world-and always the guilt and revenge and more guilt. The human is the only guilty animal. Now wait! Therefore I think this old and terrible story is important because it is a chart of the soul—the secret, rejected, guilty soul.'

"Samuel had leaned his elbows on the table and his hands covered his eyes and his forehead. 'I want to think,' he said.

"Lee said softly, 'Couldn't a world be built around accepted truth? Couldn't some pains and insanities be rooted out if the causes were known?'" **(35)**

Questions will always exist, but God made it so that not all things can be understood. Consider these questions from *The Age of Voltaire*. **(36)**

- How could the world have been created in 4004 BC when in 4000 BC China already had a developed civilization?

- Why does China have no record of Noah's flood, which according to the Bible, had covered the whole earth?

- Why had God confined his scriptural revelation to a small nation in Western Asia if he had intended it for mankind? And

- How could anyone believe that outside the church there would be no salvation? Where all those billions who had lived in India, China, and Japan—now roasting in hell?

These kinds of questions require the help of the biblical scholars! Although we can take one side or the other in the debate over the position taken by St. Paul, which concerns whether justification is achieved by faith in Christ or by works of the law, it is helpful to read the biblical scholars' account of what has caused this question to be of concern to the people and how the Bible treats the subject so that our own conclusions may be reached. St. Paul seems to be arguing with those who think that all they have to do to receive God's grace is to perform good deeds because they have already made a commitment to trust in God by having faith in Jesus. The author of James on the other hand seems to be saying there must exist a real commitment to God before man may experience and show true faith, which is the only way he can perform good works.

James writes at 2:14-26, "What good is it my brothers, if a man claims to have faith but has no deeds? Can that faith save him? If a brother or sister has nothing to wear and has no food for the day, and one of you says to them, 'Go in peace, keep warm and eat well,' but you do not give them the necessities of the body, what good is it? So also faith of itself, if it does not have works, is dead. Indeed someone might say, 'You have faith and I have works.' Demonstrate your faith to me without works, and I will demonstrate my faith to you from my works. You believe that God is one. You do well. Even the demons believe that and tremble. Do you want proof, you ignoramus, that faith without works is useless? Was not Abraham, our father, justified by works when he offered his son Isaac upon the altar? You see that faith was active along with his works, and faith was completed by the works. Thus, the scripture was fulfilled that says, 'Abraham believed God, and it was credited to him as righteousness,' and he was called the friend of God. 'See how a person is justified by works and not by faith alone.' And in the same way, was not Rahab the harlot also justified by works when she welcomed the messengers and sent them out by a different route? For just as a body without a spirit is dead, so also faith without works is dead."

We Cannot Know It All:
The interesting characteristic involving the study of religion is the incisive desire by scholars to come up with theories that will challenge the deepest thinker to stretch the realm of impossible to the brink of possibilities. Their major concern centers around creation, purpose, and value—what type of Deity is the truth, and what belief holds the most promise for mankind? Questions such as these or theories by contrast, which deal with the afterlife, for example, are not important to a Buddhist. Asian Buddhists are more interested in ethical social values and maintaining correct moral behavior. For a Buddhist, there are no threats of hell or promises of heaven. The rebirth or avoidance of the circle of life depends on one's actions on earth, body speech, and mind. The five ethical precepts and philosophical tenets of Buddhism must fulfill the command not to be violent, respecting the property of others, not giving way to lust, being truthful and honest, and respecting by not abusing the body.

Their five principal relationships include the relationships between ruler and subject, father and son, elder brother and younger brother, husband

and wife, and friend and friend. Each relationship has its own set of rules and responsibilities and are complimentary of the Noble Eightfold Path a Buddhist must follow and similar to the importance of the Ten Commandments to the Jews and to the Christian. To the Chinese, the five relationships represent the human side of their faith that have bound people and their cultures together to form the foundation for a long and continuous life for their nations and their cultures.

In Thomas W. Rhys's translation of the *Dialogues of the Buddha*, we're reminded that "not in the sky, not in the midst of the sea, not if one enters into the clefts of the mountains is there a spot in the whole world where a man may be freed from an evil deed. Hatred does not cease by hatred; hatred ceases by love. This is the eternal law." Buddha, meaning, "the enlightened one" is a title given to men of great wisdom. It is said, "To commit no evil to do all that is good, to keep one's thought pure. This is the teaching of all the Buddha's." **(37)** The Noble Eightfold Path describes the way to the end of suffering as it was laid out by Siddhartha Gautama. It is a practical guideline to ethical and mental development with the goal of freeing the individual from attachments and delusions; it finally leads to understanding the truth about all things. Together with the Four Noble Truths which are the truth of suffering, the truth of the cause of suffering, the truth of the end of suffering, and the truth of the path leading to the end of suffering. The Noble Eightfold Path and the Four Noble Truths constitute the gist of Buddhism**.** The Noble Eightfold Path consists of:

Wisdom: 1. Right view—see and understand things as they really are.
2. Right intention—commitment to ethical and mental self-improvement.
3. Right speech—abstain from false speech, no lies, not slanderous, tell the truth.

Ethical Conduct: 4. Right action to act kindly and compassionately.
5. Right livelihood—earn one's living in a righteous way.
6. Right effort—Participate in wholesome endeavors.

Mental Development: 7. Right mindfulness—see things as they are.
8. Right concentration—wholesome concentration through the practice of meditation. **(38)**

LITERATURE TEACHES SOCIAL VALUES

If there is no room in the schools for religious education, I hope our teachers will teach the human values portrayed in the world's classics. Social values are part of our religious heritage and are the subject of some of our greatest classics. Upton Sinclair's novel, for example, *The Jungle* shows the plight of immigrants during the early 1900s and what terrible working and living conditions they had to endure. It reflects how they were taken advantage, cheated, and disrespected. *The Jungle* reflects the immigrants' great courage, passion for success by working harder if necessary, staying the course at all costs, and living up to their traditional values while maintaining a moral and ethical behavior. They were often mistreated to the point of being so discouraged that giving up was becoming an option.

It was Sinclair's use of historical fiction that illustrated and condemned the atrocities he discovered in his investigative reporting of Chicago's meatpacking plants and the lives of the stockyard workers that finally caught the attention of the public. His illustrated presentations of these conditions eventually led to the passing of the Pure Food and Drug Act of 1906. By the way, Sinclair exposes the plight of the immigrants' experiences, the social injustices that they had to endure, and how they handled unscrupulous characters; one cannot only learn a lot about the actual history of the time but a lot about the integrity of these immigrants and how they survived. Upton Sinclair's portrayal of the unhealthy conditions of this industry during the early history of Chicago's meatpacking industry also led to the passing of the Meat Inspection Act. The sad thing was that the public was more concerned with the spoiled meat they were eating than the horrific working conditions of the immigrants who were eating the same food.

Literature has been responsible for bringing to light all sorts of sad conditions that people had to endure throughout time. History has explained the conditions, which authors used for their stories, while the Bible explains how these social conditions could be created. The novelists then present the consequences of society's choices.

One of my favorite character stories was written by Willa Cather. With the annexation by the United States of the former Mexican territory of New Mexico, a great opportunity to expand the U.S. Catholic See was created. Anticipating a request from the provincial council at Baltimore for the founding of an apostolic vicariate in New Mexico, three European cardinals, and an American missionary bishop met to discuss whom they should appoint to develop the new territory. Recognizing that their appointment of a new bishop to this See would "direct the beginning of momentous things." **(39) p. 6** This is the opening scene of Willa Cather's narrative, as she preferred to call it, *Death Comes for the Archbishop*. The American Missionary describes the situation the new bishop will face:

> This country was evangelized in fifteen hundred by the Franciscan Fathers. It has been allowed to drift for nearly three hundred years and is not yet dead. It still pitifully calls itself a Catholic country, and tries to keep the forms of Religion without instruction. The old mission churches are in ruins. The few Priests are without guidance or discipline. They are lax in religious observance, and some of them live in open concubinage. **(39) p. 6**

The European cardinals, not familiar with the territory, asks, "But these Missions are still under the jurisdiction of Mexico, are they not? In the See of the Bishop of Durango . . . the Bishop of Durango is an old man; and from his seat to Sante Fe is a distance of fifteen hundred English miles. There are no wagon roads, no canals, no navigable rivers. Trade is carried on by means of pack-mules, over treacherous trails. The desert down there has a peculiar horror; I do not mean thirst, nor Indian massacres, which are frequent. The very floor of the world is creaked open into countless canyons and arroyos, fissures in the earth, which are sometimes ten feet deep, sometimes a thousand. Up and down these stony chasms, the traveler and his mules clamber as best they can. It is impossible to go far in any direction without crossing them. If the Bishop of Durango should summon a disobedient priest by letter, who shall bring the Padre to him? Who can prove that he ever received the summons? The post is carried by hunters, fur trappers, gold seekers, whoever happens to be moving on the trails." **(39) p. 7**

Cather paints a pretty dim picture of the terrain, which requires a tremendous amount of time and skill to travel. This environment prompts the cardinals to conclude that the new bishop should be "a young man of strong constitution, full of zeal and above all, intelligent. He will have to deal with savagery and ignorance, with dissolute priests and political intrigue. He must be a man to whom order is necessary—as dear as life—in short it was everyone's opinion that the new territory would . . . drink up his youth and strength as it does the rain" **(39) p. 8-9** as an example of what the new bishop would face.

What is taught in *Death Comes for the Archbishop* is that we need to preserve the traditions of the past in order to protect and carry them on in an orderly and proud manner, building on those traditions with the goal of making the future more efficient. What is needed in life to support traditions is a discipline to preserve and carry them out. Without a doubt, the novel is a history of the Catholic presence in the new territory of New Mexico and Arizona from the time of the earliest missionaries of the 1600s to the latter part of the 1900s. But much more than that, it represents how the belief in a personal theology, faith in that theology, and the perseverance to accomplish a goal is what carries on a tradition that builds the future. As Cather points out in her wonderful novel, the Mexicans saw this conquest of their home differently. Overnight, they had become a minority with a different language, culture, and laws. The church's role in this experience as told in Cather's work shows how important contributions can be made by many cultures for the food of its community so that a new culture can be created. The U.S. invaders who were made of many cultural backgrounds, Mexicans, and Indians became Americans. Catholics and spiritual superstitions had blended in a way that the past was preserved, the present had indeed been created, and the future under God's care would be blessed. With a spirit of religious faith, Cather has showed in her novel how young men full of zeal, with a strong constitution, and above all, intelligence can deal with savagery and ignorance and restore order to an unorderly wild environment when guided by God's will.

Imagination Sometimes Becomes Real

Picture this: you are sitting under the shade of an oak tree one clear and sunny morning. You smile and marvel at the beauty that surrounds you. Trees and flowers complement the landscape, and decorating the skies are small white clouds with colorful birds darting in and out. All of a sudden, you notice rabbits with their young, playing in the tall grass nearby. You can hear the sound of water falling over rocks from above into the smaller clear blue pool below. You begin to think that this earth is so beautiful, clean, and filled with innocents. The flowers have such a sweet aroma, and the trees seem to be guarding the rolling countryside like soldiers guarding a treasure. How did it all get here you think? Why am I here? Why do people destroy beauty? And why do the innocent have to suffer? You begin to recall all the stories you have been told about the "creation." Your mind starts to create images; you are a "Genesis" writer.

When you think about it, how does a theory mature? How would you research or get answers to your questions when there are no libraries or no one to consult or discuss the possibilities you think your theory may produce because there has never been anyone who has given any thought to the subject? When you have questions about a subject that has never been considered as being relative or is considered to be beyond one's comprehension, you must begin to realize that you will be the one to develop answers, but you can't be sure they are correct. Your theories may be ridiculous to some, of no concern to others, but interesting to those who are deep thinkers. You know, because of the very nature of oral tradition, that your original thoughts will get changed and your ideas will seem to present different conclusions; but still, you proceed to challenge your psyche and work to appeal to the reasonableness that are willing to work toward the development of an acceptable conclusion.

As people become interested in finding their own answers to the questions you've raised, it's possible your original theory may develop into a whole other approach or discovery. To those who have studied your ideas, their minds will start to reason things out for themselves. Sooner or later, your story may even get changed beyond recognition; and with the passing of time, new ideas and theories will be born for others to consider based on your original thoughts. There is also a great probability that sometime, far into the future, someone called an editor might come along to choose from many additional theories that have been presented since your conclusions were first written and rewrite what he thought you must have meant. This may occur long after you are gone; he may decide that his ideas are more reasonable than yours are, based on the information now available that you did not have at the time. He may even rewrite what you had concluded, based on this new information, calling it a more accurate account of what did or did not happen and why. Some questions we will never have answers for, just like we will never know the length of infinity or where God came from, why the innocent suffer, and why some take advantage of opportunities and some don't.

Consider Being a Part of What Your Church Thinks You Should Be: Bringing it all together will make you happier. Your house of the Lord, with all its rituals and beliefs, should be loved, supported, and defended—just as a loving father loves his family. The church experience makes one aware of possible alternatives when faced with choices that create anxiety and doubt. It can keep one focused on desired goals and help cure the feeling of depression. Depression, according to Father Athanasius Iskander, is the "closest thing to being in hell" and one of the most crucial mental problems people suffer. In a PowerPoint presentation to his congregation at St. Mary's church in Kitchener, Canada, on the Seven Trumpets from Revelation, Father Iskander tells his audience that "'depression' is a state of utter hopelessness where the present is worse than the past, and the future is even worse than the present. The torment and mental agony are so overpowering that the only deliverance often seems to be death."

Father Iskander suggests that the main reason for this epidemic is that people are increasingly estranged from the grace of God. He quotes Dr. Margaret Somerville of the McGill Centre for Medicine, Ethics, and Law in Montreal who thinks, "Medicine has become our substitute religion. If you're treating your spiritual yearnings with Prozac, you have a problem haven't you?" **(40)** While God is responsible for all the people on this earth, people are responsible for what they believe. People can be something, nothing, or something in between. When you study God's Word in His house of worship, you learn what specific responsibilities are expected to be fulfilled. "In many cultures there is no distinction between religion and everyday life. People simply see themselves as living according to the ways and wisdom of their people and traditions. Muslims for example, say that Islam is not a religion—it is a way of life. Most Hindus do not realize they 'belong' to that religion, for it is a name given by outsiders." **(41)**

What people in the West mean by "religion" is often seen by other cultures as a narrow perception of the role of God and of humanity.

This distinction between secular society and religion in the West, expressed in the separation of church and state in the American and other constitutions, is impossible for many of the peoples of the world to understand. "Life is faith and faith is life."

Perhaps this is a philosophy we need to practice in our Christian churches to get the man in the pew to act and think the same during the week as he does on Sunday?

God's house gives its believers a head start toward a healthy moral life. The house of the Lord is an inspirational experience, which lights the flames of ethics and morality. The church endorses a unified belief that supports moral character and acts in favor of the common good. The church makes us better citizens. The church eases our pain, is forgiving, and lessens the worry of death. The church experience encourages you to learn all that you can absorb about your theology. You should, therefore, learn what it teaches; you should respect it and live it. For example, before I made a serious attempt to learn about my religion, theology meant the study of God, now it means, faith looking for understanding. It involves participation, which I think is the best way to experience "the study of God."

It is unfortunate that the word *church* has the same connotation to some as "school" has to many students. They question, "Do I have to go?" Alternatively, "Why do we have to learn this stuff?" Their protest is heard all too often, and frankly, I think parents could be more supportive in their answers to this attitude rather than relying on old clichés like, "You need to graduate to make something of yourself!" Or, "It won't hurt you to go to church. It might do you some good."

The young person who attends school or church with the attitude that if he goes through the motions he will survive this awful experience is fooling himself and will eventually disappoint others. The sad thing is, they will probably somehow accomplish their goal; but people survive automobile crashes and heart attacks too. The point is, if they do not change, an undesirable event will eventually take place. What they do not understand is, if information learned by experience, school, church, and oral tradition presents us with choices, we need our church and educational knowledge to help us make the best choice we can make from the information we have received. The difference between a learned person and someone with arrogance for formal education is their clear defiance for authority and their lack of concern for the common good. While they may have talent yet unexplored to accomplish worthy goals, their attitude to learn is confined to the methods they choose to learn by which is not always complementary to the result they achieve. Proverbs 12:15 explains, "The way of the fool seems right in his own eyes but he who listens to advice is wise."

In our democratic society, people have the freedom to exchange ideas freely and create rules of law, which apply to everyone equally. Choosing leaders and establishing policies requires comprehensive citizen participation. This task, however, requires a tremendous amount of thought, debate, and cooperation. The church community, with all its ministries and social projects, recommends that cooperation becomes a necessary characteristic of its leaders and committee organizers.

The duties and responsibilities of society's citizens are demanding if we are to have a good government. Citizens who become policy makers must maintain a respect for diversity, posses a knowledge, which is sympathetic to the needs of the majority and in the best interest of its people regardless of their race, religion, or political beliefs. Few people are qualified to represent the majority on these conditions; therefore, it is very important for citizens to be of good moral character and support those with proven integrity. If one cannot contribute, one can work on their campaign, encourage others to vote, and promote their candidacy in conversations. It's important to know what elected officials are doing and what policies they are promoting so that your voiced opinion can have an influence. To protect your rights to the maximum, you must also be prepared to respect the opinions of others even if you disagree with their conclusions. In this multicultural society, respecting the opinions of others regardless of race, religion, beliefs, or other differences has the potential of creating an atmosphere, which is more conducive to compromise instead of hostility. Each week, in your house of the Lord, learn to walk humbly with your God and be reminded what the right thing to do is: that which benefits the common good and the church.

Maybe the question has become, what makes it difficult for us to connect our prayers with our living? Maybe we are not living our life the way Jesus expects us to. Sometimes we make it hard to connect prayer with the way we live. Then again, maybe it's because our love is not "on course" with God's way or expectations. I'm not sure that very many truly understand how to pray, even though most of us understand what the sources of prayers are, i.e., the Word of God, the liturgy of the church, and the virtues of faith, hope, and love. Sometimes we should take time to question whether our motives are such that we are expecting God to make it happen without any special or sacrificial effort on our part. Our faith should grow stronger when we pray to God, and if our motives are for the good of the community, we can only hope that they are suitable requests to receive God's blessings.

THINGS TO THINK ABOUT!

The Origin of Our Religious Experience and Knowledge

1. Parents
2. Sunday school
3. Family traditions
4. Our own conclusions
5. What we read and how we interpret it
6. Academic sources
7. Belief in our actions
8. Opinions of peers
9. Results of our experiences
10. FAITH

WHY SHOULD WE BECOME PART OF A WORSHIPING FAMILY?

1. Nothing can ever give one more pleasure than walking with Jesus through the passages of Matthew, Mark, Luke, and John.

2. The church family experience can help us:
   - stay focused on attaining goals,
   - overcome depression and lessen hostility,
   - to know what our responsibilities should be,
   - to be a better citizen, to build a moral and ethical character.

3. The church offers us the opportunity to participate in social ministries, which
   - encourages participation in community projects;
   - promotes, by example, the meaning of compromise;
   - creates in us a concern for doing what's right for the common good;
   - provides many opportunities to learn
     - about church history,
     - the New and Old Testament,
     - the liturgy and its origins,
     - other faiths.

The church teaches us the importance and value of prayer and our statements of what we believe as Christians: the Lord's Prayer, Apostles' Creed, and the Nicene Creed are like the mortar that gives the wall its strength. These things make our faith unbreakable.

The decision to become a member of a church family, which respects the gift of life of course, is yours to make. This is the freedom we have been given. Without statements of beliefs to guide us, we have no religion, no church, and no country. As we continue to move away from the principles taught in all Christian, Muslim, or Jewish faiths, as we continue to mock moral integrity and reflect a character with little respect for life and integrity, we will continue to neglect the responsibilities Jesus asked us to perform and the results of an Armageddon will get closer.

In the spirit of St. Paul in Galatians 3:2-5, Consider this, if you have developed a statement of beliefs, where did the spirit for your beliefs come from? Regardless of what the beliefs you follow may be, what was their origin? From the laws that force you under penalty of death or confinement to obey or from the wisdom of thoughts tried and proven to be in the best interest of all. Do the laws that you follow require you to have faith to believe in them or the performance of works so you can see the results? Micah said, "You have been told, O man, what is good, and what the Lord requires of you; Only to do the right and to love goodness, and to walk humbly with your God."

You may remember, from an earlier chapter, when I talked about Henry Fleming in Stephen Crane's *The Red Badge of Courage* telling his mama he was going to enlist in the army and what her advice to him was for this decision: "Henry," she says, "don't think of anything 'cept what's right . . . and the Lord'll take keer of us all." She proceeds to advise him the importance of keeping his socks mended and clean and then very proudly gives him a little Bible saying, "There'll be many a time, too Henry when yeh'll be wanting advice, boy, and all like that, and there'll be nobody round, perhaps, to tell yeh things. Then if you take it out, boy, yeh'll find wisdom in it, Henry—with little or no searching." **(42)**

May God be with you!

Chapter Six

Learn All You Can

When Jesus commissioned the apostles to build His church, they were "ignited by the resurrection and fueled by the Holy Spirit, as a result, the church grew in—all directions geographically as well as socially. Jesus had sent His disciples into the entire world and St. Paul had opened the church to Gentiles. In a sense, Christianity was simply a development of Jesus' plans and St. Paul's efforts." **(1)**

In Jesus's time, those who worshiped gods and idols outnumbered Christians. Most of the population was Jewish and included the territories from Egypt to Russia and from Britain to Arabia. The people were different culturally and socially, spoke different languages, and maintained different opinions about how things should be done. It was not until the reign of Constantine (from AD 313-337) that Christianity became the official religion of the Roman Empire, but it took the Reformation in the sixteenth century, the Nicene Creed, and the Apostles' Creed to unite the Protestant and Catholic Christians.

Based on the hope that there would be religious freedom, land for farming, and better opportunities, the great migration from Europe to the United States spread Christians in all directions. While they were exploring new ideas and developing different ways of doing things, it was these "statement of beliefs" that kept the church together and the Declaration of Independence that united all citizens of this new country politically. You often hear speakers referring to what history will say about an event. When we examine the word *history* we notice it contains within it the difference between the things that happened in the past, which are recoded and documented, and the stories we tell about the past, handed down by oral tradition from generation to generation. History focuses on the written record of human experience, revealing how individuals and societies resolved their problems and sometimes how they made things worst. History discloses the consequences of choices that were made. The religious statements of belief contained in the Nicene Creed and the Apostles' Creed, along with the Declaration of Independence, written for the benefit of the common good, became the documents that made this new land the greatest country in the world.

By establishing religious freedom, an educational system providing learning experiences for everyone, a political democracy representing all citizens, support for the arts, and a demonstrated respect for the earth and its habitants, Americans improved the quality of lives for all their citizens for years to come. As a new country, fighting for and protecting their rights, Americans quickly learned that good leadership was the building blocks of establishing a strong and ethically sound society. They also knew that it would be the moral and ethical behavior resulting from their religious backgrounds that would protect the integrity of their beliefs. They understood the responsibility they had, as parents, to teach their future leaders to love and value God, their country, and family. The first migration of Americans knew that the future would depend on the honest integrity and godly morality, which was in the hearts of their sons and daughters. To be successful, they recognized the value of what happened at home, to encourage their young people to achieve academic successes and to become enthusiastic about acquiring the vocational skills and knowledge to provide food, clean water, and the necessary mechanical and technical tools needed to keep our great country healthy and making it progressively better, would be necessary. Adults, with or without children, realized the importance of practicing Christian principles at home, at work, and at play by making fair and sound decisions in their everyday dealings. They knew this behavior would demonstrate to their sons and daughter their sincere devotion to maintaining a disciplined and godly behavior to immolate. They encouraged family participation in church activities and became involved in community issues until they were resolved.

I think parents today have the same obligation as our early American forefathers to live a godly life and to encourage their sons and daughters to develop their interest to the fullest. Parents should encourage their young people to participate in as many activities as they can at school, in church, and in their community. School activities such as DECA which originally meant Distributive Education Clubs of America but is now called an Association of Marketing Students, sports, chorus, cheerleading, band, orchestra, and special interest clubs such as the Latin, French, Spanish, and Biology and mentally challenging activities such as debate, chess, and socially oriented activities such as producing a yearbook, tutoring pals, and student council should be encouraged. All of these activities promote teamwork and help build attitudes of fair play and good sportsmanship, which are so important, not only in today's competitive working arena, but also in the maturing of proper social behavior. If young people must work to help the family survive, because of today's economy, there are ministries in church which they could belong that would provide them with a sense of accomplishment, value, and experience with very little time requirements.

Community-Based Organizations:
If it is at all possible, parents should encourage young people to participate in activities, which are community based as well, such as 4-H, Future Farmers of America, the National Association of Christian Athletes, or Scouting. Special people called volunteers are always needed in hospitals, nursing homes, Habitat for Humanity, or the Jesus House. All of these activities and organizations promote the concept of the common good, endorse social justice, and promote the importance of charity. The good news is, in order for students to participate in activities such as these, they are required to maintain a grade point average that reflects their ability to maintain academic accomplishments. A student who is active in school, church, and community activities, while maintaining a grade point average adequate enough to receive recognition from teachers and administrators, will bring them invitations and scholarships for pursuing other learning opportunities. The student who accomplishes these things will be recognized by his school, church, and community like a who's who among students and will be too busy to be involved with Satan-driven vices.

Aren't Students Taking Advantage of All There Is to Offer? Largely, many students are participating in these kinds of activities and are taking advantage of everything their school, church, and community have to offer. The problem I see in today's schools is that there are not enough students who appreciate the value of doing extra things to enhance their character, interests, and ultimately their success. Going to school is something the law requires them to do, and learning is something that must be done in order to pass on to the next phase of life. Many students do not see learning as something necessary in order to become an asset to society or to improve their individual skills; they see learning as a requirement to get a job. Although this may not be the case with the advanced student, I think all too often their willingness to participate is inspired by parents who know how Advance Placement classes and extra special activities will look on their student's résumé and what extra benefits they will receive in the way of scholarships or other recognition.

What Are the Problems: Teachers must deal with problems daily. Things neither they nor the school district has any control over such as a lack of money due to failed bond proposals and governmental mandated requirements which require specific materials, additional reading specialists, special education teachers, and math teachers. Some of the more common problems include the following:

- An increasing number of illegal immigrants who expect a free public education for their children.

- As our country becomes more culturally mixed, teachers must deal with many students who have difficulty speaking our language, accepting authority, or have not yet learned the necessary social skills required to achieve and maintain acceptable behavior in the classroom.

- All too often, teachers are challenged to deal with two personalities at the same time: those that do want to learn and those who do not want to learn. Our ivory tower educators suggest that their exposure to a better educational climate will encourage them to want to learn. The truth is, the less talented academically the kids are, the less they seem to care whether they learn or not because they lose interest and are discouraged more quickly. The result is that the better students suffer, not only because of the slower student's disruptive behavior, but also because the material is presented in a repetitive, slower, and more boring pace. Some parents are encouraging kids to go to work instead of school. They think to learn to earn is better than learning how to add, subtract, multiply, or think constructively. This attitude creates a great deal of attendance problems. No kid in school to teach makes it hard to keep test scores high when combined with those who don't care about learning or come to school.

- Discipline is becoming a problem in a lot of classrooms, which requires the support of the parents to correct. Today's administration, all too often, seems to bow to the scorn of parents who think their child has been mistreated some way or another instead of working with the teacher and parent to solve the problem.

- In some schools, there are not enough classrooms. When no temporary buildings are available, teachers are given large carts to push around with their books and other teaching materials on it from room to room. This is not only tiring for the teacher, but also displays to the students what someone in authority thinks of the importance of providing the proper equipment and learning environment for their education.

- The state and federal government has demanded through the No Child Left Behind Act that certain required levels of reading skills be obtained. The problem is, the law does not take into consideration variances in learning abilities of those required to achieve these results. Surely, we all must know that students who are coming together as one group from an omnibus background will possess learning abilities that stager from very capable to somewhat questionable.

- The lack of funds causes hardships on everyone within the educational process. In some districts, teachers who have enough service time accumulated to retire are being asked to take early retirement. Principals will have to give up two to three days wages to save money while support personnel are being asked to voluntarily forgo two to three days wages. When there is a budget shortfall, educational employees are not the only ones who suffer, how about the students? They no longer have the experienced teachers to teach them, disgruntled administrators lose a little incentive, and support personnel who make things clean, students fed, and keep facilities in good shape become discouraged. Education is always conceived as being necessary, and it is always agreed that we need to support our schools, but something always happens to cause the budget to be short. In the best of times and in the worst of times, since 1966 when I first started in the education business, the story has not changed: no money, teachers aren't doing a good enough job, low wages for everyone, there is always a lack of materials to teach with, facilities to learn in, and equipment to make the job a little more efficient. Maybe it is time our schools were run like a business. Surely, the overhead would be cut; and *proficiency* would be a word that would apply to administrators, boards of education, and parents. Cuts would apply to the number of school districts in a state and not just teachers.

Thinking Should Be a Part of the Educational Process:
In today's classroom, students expect A's without much effort. Teachers and parents do not seem to have the time to promote an atmosphere of curiosity in the student to develop question-asking skills, which are so important in the communications process at school and home. Parents are too busy keeping the mortgage paid, and teachers must teach to pass the test to worry about anything else. Soon, students who lack the ability to think will produce enough of a concern that it will be added to the list of things society and the government can blame teachers for not accomplishing. "In most cases, schooling does not develop curiosity; delight in ambiguity, and question-asking skills. Rather, the thinking skill that's rewarded is figuring out the 'Right Answer'—that is, the answer held by the person in authority, the teacher." "Curiosity" and creative problem solving are a concept credited to the genius of Leonardo de Vinci's seven principles of learning. "Curiosity" promotes the quest for continuous learning by always maintaining a curious commitment to asking questions and continual learning. **(2)**

I agree that learning should be an exercise in thinking and should promote the efficiency of one's mind. However, with today's mandated proficiency requirements, the pressure and demands by parents for their kid to make A's, colleges and universities increasing their cost and entrance requirements because there are so many more qualified applicants today, is causing schools and students to follow a course that will soon go afoul. In my opinion, combining skills with the willingness to cooperate and the ability to multitask with on-the-job team members accomplishes more toward getting the job successfully completed than knowing a bunch of facts that are readily available by accessing the proper source. Just recently, an article in our local newspaper supports this conclusion. In response to a request from a large human resource placement firm to prepare a survey listing of the most important qualities sought by firms today, the results showed: On a scale from 1-10, with 10 being the highest, professionalism ranked 9.2, critical thinking was 8.5, and written communications was 8.2. Other skills ranking high on the list of important qualities that workers should posses included ethics, teamwork, and English-language skills. (**3**) Researcher Leslie Hart says, after a classic study at a top university was done, it seems the summa cum laude graduates were given their final exams one month after graduation, and they all failed. "Final exams are final indeed! The bottom line summary to this is:

"The authority pleasing, (**parents / and educational institution**)

question—suppressing, (**teacher**)

rule following approach to education, (**Pass the test at all costs**)

may have served to provide society with assembly line workers and bureaucrats, but it does not do much to prepare us for a new Renaissance."

The Sad Facts:
Even though the emphasis is on teaching to pass the test, score high on SAT's, and increase graduation statistics, according to an article in *U.S. News & World Report*, the author, Alex Kingsbury reports that "nationwide, only 63 percent of entering freshman will graduate from college within six years." Derek Bok, former Harvard president and the author of *Our Underachieving College* says, every college try to do what the brochure says, "To help students reach their full potential," yet, according to Kingsbury's article, only 31 percent of college graduates can read texts and draw inferences at a proficient level. Fewer than half of all college students, other studies show, graduate with broad proficiency in math and reading. And according to Bok, evidence suggests that several groups of college students, particularly blacks and Hispanics,

consistently underperform levels expected of them given their SAT scores and high school grades.

Isn't it reasonable to expect a college graduate to be somewhat capable of thinking? Shouldn't it be reasonable to expect college graduates, after spending thousands of dollars, to be proficient at comparing and contrasting ideas and concepts relative to their major subject of study, to be able to converse in one foreign language, to have a minimum conversational knowledge of U.S. and World History, to be familiar with the literary classics, appreciate the arts, and maintain an appreciation of other cultures along with an interest in continuing to learn as much as possible about their major subject of interest? College graduates, or for that matter, high school graduates, should be able to analyze a given set of facts in a critical and logical method, maintain respect for diverse cultures, and have excellent communication skills in their native language. They should be, to some degree, able to display a sense of enthusiasm for the ability to speak in a foreign tongue thereby reflecting an appreciation of others who have mastered their native language. Teaching to pass tests doesn't seem to be working.

Parents who raise their voices in protest to everyone from the janitor to the administration, if their student receives a C instead of an A, needs to live for a while in the real world and think about the capabilities, interests, and motivation of their sons and daughters; maybe they should communicate with them by having an intellectual conversation with them. Kenneth C. Davis's *Don't Know Much about History* tells about a 1987 survey of high school juniors that exposed astonishing gaps in what seventeen year olds knew about American History and literature. Davis writes, "A third of the students couldn't identify the Declaration of Independence as the document that marked the formal separation of the thirteen colonies from Great Britain. Only thirty two percent of the students surveyed could place the American Civil War in the correct half century." **(4)**

Why Do We Have To Learn This Stuff Anyway?
One very frequent, under-the-breath comment I heard every year from students was, "Why do we have to learn this stuff?" It really doesn't matter what "this stuff" is because the diversity found in each class is such that there will always be someone who doesn't like something. Therefore, teachers have the challenge to make the subject interesting

and use creative teaching methods so the students won't think what they are doing is too much work and dismiss it as being too hard. Learning must be fun for them, or it won't sink in with their idea of usefulness. I agree, learning can and should be fun, but in my opinion, one must work hard to achieve success and most things worth accomplishing are not easy, including learning. Sorry, but learning requires some hard work.

If seven out of ten understand the material to the point they can apply what they've learned, two won't have a clue what it is about and one could care less what it's about—regardless of how hard you try to teach them by using all the creative means available. The point is, we are bound to remember that all ten students are God's children and must be respected. We are reminded to remember that teaching solely to prepare students for college is not and should not be our major goal. We need to teach students to be able to acquire the skills needed to apply what they have learned in order to accomplish a satisfactory result in their area of endeavor; but first, they must be able to pass the test.

A very bright student may want to be the business manager of a car dealership or a master technician of a small appliance retail store he hopes to own. Others may even want to be a master chef. We also have to realize that, for now, there are some who simply what to say, "Would you like fries with that?" Getting a job is a topic that students can talk about forever, and when they do, the amount of money earned is what represents whether they have been successful or not and not what grade they made in your class. It was Bernard Lonergan who said, "Teaching focuses responsibility and nurtures it; it does not create or impose it." **(5)**

I recently asked a high school graduate, in her second year of vocational school, what subjects, clubs, or things learned in high school were helping her in life today. Interestingly, she was quick to point out that DECA had been the most helpful because she had learned things such as how to complete an application for employment, what to say at an interview, how to market products, etc. Core subjects were not mentioned. I found the same results to be true when I talked to students who had been out of school for several years and had been involved in subjects dealing with consumerism, family life, street law, industrial arts, stagecraft, etc. Could it be that interest in learning is directly related to the immediate results obtained or whether or not it's easy and fun?

College-bound students remember facts and subject matter from core courses because they are required to know them in order to succeed in college; jobs and life skills come later. One thing is for sure, their social skills when having parties and good times far exceed their noncollege peers. I think this is because most students who are interested in running their own business, for example, are more interested in how to deal with life and business situations the minute they walk out the graduation door. Courses like business math, bookkeeping, computer programming, and marketing all benefit them immediately. Math skills come closest to the interest of all because of its relevance in everyday activities.

What Should the Role of the Educator Be?
In a February 21, 2005 edition of *Time* magazine there is an article entitled, "Parents Behaving Badly." In this article, the author, Nancy Gibbs proceeds to explain the conflict that exists between parents and teachers in today's classroom. She describes teachers as "combatants getting ready for battle." She characterizes parents as "passionate, protective creatures when it comes to their children, as nature designed them to be." On the other hand, she points out that "teachers strive to be dispassionate objective professionals, as their training requires them to be." I have observed many situations develop because of attitudes. When you deal with all those who are concerned with class and race, combined with kids today who have been taught to question authority, and a public who thinks the schools should take care of all their parenting problems—teach those who do not want to learn, teach those who can't understand English, and demand that the schools and teachers be more accountable for how kids perform—Ms. Gibbs concludes, as do I, it is a miracle that parents and teachers get along as well as they do.

The situation is so bad that 73 percent of new teachers, according to a recent educational pole, quoted in her article say, "Too many parents treat schools and teachers as adversaries." I saw a high school principal get so mad at a parent for criticizing his school and one of his teachers that he lost control of his temper and said some things in retaliation to the parent's obnoxious behavior. Because this person went to the news media with a story less than the truth, he was disciplined by the district administration. I have heard student teachers say, "This is not for me," leave the classroom, and change majors. I had a ninth grader cry because she was concerned what her mother was going to say to her for making a C on a vocabulary test. You dare not surprise a student by giving an unannounced quiz, regardless of your purpose. God forbid if you do something in the curriculum that was not announced days before. If you are going to have a test, you have to give them the questions in advance so they can look up the answers. This is called the Review Study Guide. After they have had an opportunity to memorize the answers, you can select some of the questions for your test. Kids are so conditioned to be regimented that thinking and reacting to change is like speaking a foreign language to them. They have a terrible time coping with change and are quick to tell you that this is not the way we do it as if they are teaching the class. Students today are so lazy they fail open book tests! Some of them have no clue what awaits them when they are finally able to leave school, with or with a certificate of having attended a public high school, but the bright students find most core subjects a "give me an A" class and boring.

I think teachers do a terrific job in today's environment. What they have to put up with is frustrating to be sure, but the biggest disappointment to the creative teacher is to have to teach to pass tests. Only the Advanced Placement teachers have the best students and can be creative in their presentations of the material they are teaching while some even make students think! I always feel bad for those students who have to be placed in a classroom with those few who try to constantly be disruptive, who lack any evidence of interest, and who behave in a manner that distracts the attention the teacher can offer others who want to learn. Students are provided with every tool available to make their experience a learning achievement, but some just do not want to take advantage of any opportunity they are presented. I saw a poster in an eighth grade history classroom recently that defined *diversity*.

It read: D = different
         I = individuals
         V = valuing
         E = each other
         R = regardless of
         S = skin
         I = intellect
         T = talents or

Y = years

The poster did not credit the author, but I credit the teacher for having the wisdom to display it and for teaching its principles while serving as an example of its message.

Among the many opportunities available to a variety of students today is, of course, the Web. In an article entitled, "Web Offers Unique Schooling Style," the author, Wendy K. Kleinman, a staff writer for our local newspaper says, "More than 1,000 middle and high school students in Oklahoma take classes online, with some earning their diplomas solely through online schoolwork." As to the type of students who participate, Kleinman says, "Students include those who are accelerated academically, pursuing talents in arts and athletics, business entrepreneurs, rural students seeking a wider range of choices, homeschoolers who want a diploma, living with chronic medical conditions, teenage parents and dropouts." The more talented student can earn as many as fifteen semester hours of college credits while they are still in high school by enrolling in various university-sponsored Internet courses. It's obvious the future has exciting things in store for those who are willing to work and are prepared to go to class each day. I think it is sad to see so many of today's students wasting their time by taking no interest in learning as much as they can. Being satisfied to get by will only bring mediocrity to our society. Doing the least possible to get out of school does not prepare them for any kind of future success, but then, maybe they do not measure success by the same standards as those who want to accomplish extraordinary things.

Literature Covers Every Subject There Is and Has Been Responsible for Creating New Laws:
Accomplishments are only things some students hear about or dream about. I have always felt that a lot can be accomplished in literature class. To me, literature deals with the world of ideas and relationships in human terms. It is an account of how people behave, how they perceive their actions to be, could be, or should be. It is a fantasy come true, a chance to become what others are. Literature is the adventure that dreams are made of but never happens in our real world. When we study literature, we get to travel, become daredevils, famous, and rich. Exciting

people from faraway places surround us and as well as those that seem like they live just around the corner. Literature can be our make-believe world. We can discover great things, solve mysteries that no one else is capable of, and become the greatest at whatever our imagination wants us to be. In our fantasies—after reading about such greats as Babe Ruth, President Lincoln, Louis Pasteur, General George Washington, and Jim Thorpe—we can march in the victory parade just as they did as a celebrity. For those who want to learn more about what interests them, literature can become a world they never thought existed. Many stories deal with the theme of good and evil, teaching us what can happen when we make bad choices while others show us the benefits of making good choices and help us to recognize the advantages of developing a clean moral character. Literature has been responsible for bringing to light social injustices that have occurred in our lifetime and have aided in procuring laws to change immoral and socially unacceptable behavior.

Mother Jones was one of the most famous. Born in Ireland, Mother Jones became known as the Miner's Angel for her work to secure better working conditions for miners. Her work for children's rights and child labor laws made her feared by big business. She was a leader of all leaders when it came to fighting for social justice issues. She was quoted as saying, "Pray for the dead and fight like Hell for the living."

All of life's struggles can be experienced in the classics of American literature. I can't think of a better way to teach or challenge young minds than for them to learn about and experience the thematic values of social justice principles than by exploring the world as represented in literature. To learn the difference between outer material success and spiritual success and to face diversity with dignity and grace are lessons that can be a lifelong benefit from studying literature. For example, exploring the dignity of the human person as a social asset is the main theme of Jon Hassler's imaginary Midwestern world. A menagerie of small town folks coming of age populates his work. Growing old and looking for bits of meaning amidst the tedium, anxieties, and absurdities of life in places where you keep running into the same neighbors or colleagues repeatedly. *Dear James* and *North of Hope* are two of my favorites.

Short stories are great character studies as well. The more profound the dilemma, in which the hero finds himself, the more one can sympathize with each character caught in the turmoil of the inner conflict. When students understand the situations that place protagonist in various positions, the better they can understand what has to be accomplished to regain his status as a hero and what got them there originally. When the story is one, which causes the reader to reflect on an internal struggle he himself has had, the interest to resolve the dilemma for the character is increased, and the means used to accomplish this is remembered. To find the inner struggle within the characters makes it easier to project alternatives for them to follow. If a student recognizes and admits to a problem or a character flaw, it is easier for him to develop alternative behavior that will resolve the conflict. As I learned in my English methods course, searching questions help the most in revealing to the student the elements that make problem solving more meaningful. "What does this story mean in my life? How does it help me to become a more mature, responsible person? What handicap is there in my personality that I can overcome as the hero did? Are there people around me that this story can help me to understand? Can it help me to understand my parents, my friends, and my school? These questions and many others like them are always more rewarding and fruitful in the study of literature than the whole armament of literary criticism." **(6)**

Another world of excitement can be found in our history books. History, unlike novels, focuses on the written record of human experiences, revealing how individuals and societies resolve their problems and discloses the consequences of their choices. However, when combined with literature, history can come alive when a relevant story explains how people were treated, conquered, or celebrated. It is the past with an example. We can learn what caused the many civil rights laws to be on the books by reading Harper Lee's *To Kill A Mockingbird*, which tells the story of how prejudice existed in the south during the '60s. It was always my belief that literature could reach, in some way or another, all students. As an active teacher, I worked very closely with my friend who taught history. If he were covering the civil war, for example, I would teach *The Red Badge of Courage*. If he were covering social discrimination during the '50s or '60s, I would teach *To Kill a Mockingbird*. I wanted students to be exposed and experience as much of history and life as possible without the hardship of having to feel the circumstances and living with the results that life's history sometimes presented. If my friend was looking at the two world wars, we would try to cover *Under Fire*, which deals with the effects of war on French soldiers of 1914-1916; or *All Quiet on the Western Front*, an intensely human but painfully realistic novel about Hitler's army; or Hemingway's *A Farewell to Arms*, a love story that takes place during the First World War in Italy. A novel, I enjoyed teaching, was the story of two priest and their missionary efforts during the developmental days of America's Southwest called *Death Comes for the Archbishop* by Willa Cather.

Since teenagers are usually interested in being in love, a story like John Galsworthy's *The Apple Tree*, which shows the conflicts and hurt that can follow when social classes are mixed, or Tolstoy's *Anna Karenina*—a tragic story of Anna's love for her son, hatred for her husband, fear of losing the man she loved, and finally, self-destruction—seemed to cover all areas of their interests. When students were studying the life and times of the early American settlers, our literature class just had to read *The Scarlet Letter* by Nathaniel Hawthorne. Some critics call this the greatest American novel written. The question in the novel deals with satirizing the Puritan conception of sin as well as the psychological effects of sin.

The goal, in this type of model, was to develop in students an interest in critically examining those character traits, which caused the character to act or react as they did in the novel. (1) By analyzing the morals, ethics, and integrity reflected in the actions of the characters, my hope was the student would better understand the benefits of having a more acceptable behavior, routed in a more socially acceptable moral and ethical character, than the one formed by the less attractive influence or to want to emulate the character of the most benevolent character. (2) I hoped to encourage an eagerness to tackle new assignments by creating challenges that would require careful thought about how the author developed character, in particular, how the protagonist's character was different from the others and what the author was trying to portray.

For example, an assignment could involve rewriting a scene from something recently read such as *The Apple Tree*. The instructions for the project could be like this: Rewrite the scene from *The Apple Tree* that tells how Frank discovers Megan has killed herself because of him. Show how you would make Frank justify to himself what he did. Make your scene reveal whether you think Frank is evil or hateful or simply made a bad choice. Include what factors Frank should have considered before saying he would marry Megan in the first place, and what was missing from his character to forsake her? What in his character made him hide from her? Is Frank the kind of guy you would want in your foxhole to cover your back in battle? The goal in making such an assignment was to encourage student to think about what in the life of this character made him do what he did, and what changes could have prevented him from causing her death or supported his behavior. What character compromises should one consider when making characters reach decisions that affect most people? If students made their character reach decisions, which were in the best interest of everyone involved, the process in formulating those conclusions or procedures would usually have to reflect some degree of compromise on everyone's part in order to create a fair and just conclusion of the problem.

I want to know what character traits one should posses that would make a person compassionate or hateful to others. To change an attitude usually required an act of understanding how the previous behavior was wrong in the eyes of a godly society or right in the eyes of a corrupt, immoral community. To want to produce a more just and tolerant result became an exercise in the students' thinking constructively about his own character. The project was intended to psychologically create a recognition pattern in the development of character that he should follow to accomplish the most good. It was my hope that exercises like these made students more enlightened and interested in increasing their desire for developing acceptable moral and ethical character traits, such as respect for all human kind. In my classes, I would always anticipate that I could encourage everyone who participated to realize that it is only when ethical, moral, and social justice principles are practiced in light of one's faith in God that a more tolerate and cooperative society could result.

The End Result:
Our society urgently needs the everyday witness of Christians who take seriously the meaning of the words *ethical, moral, social justice, right,* and *wrong.* For it is these concepts, when practiced in light of our Christian faith, that produces a society which understands and accepts responsibility for its actions and one that opens its hearts to God with little to be concerned about thereby creating an atmosphere conducive

to living with other people and promoting the dignity of all persons. I think it would be nice if we could produce a society that would always practice morally acceptable principles. If citizens would accept the responsibilities of their choices and work to produce a life that would benefit the common good, I think we would have a more congenial and stronger community. Wouldn't it be nice if everybody could feel their life changing for the better by taking an active part in a social ministry that would promote love instead of prejudice, economic justice as opposed to greed, and one which would work to give better options for the poor? If we will work to improve life by choosing to practice moral and ethical integrity when making the decisions that affects the common good, then all of us would be contributing to a happier, healthier, and more productive United States, and in turn, make life more rewarding for all people in the free world. I wanted to know from students, what in the end would make an alternative lifestyle work or not work for the protagonist? What event or trait did he/she possess that caused the story to end as it did? If you were writing this story, what would you have changed? Why?

Communications Makes the World Go Round; Sharing What We Know:
This leads us to the end. But I must ask, what is all this worth if we cannot communicate our feelings, write a report for our employer, write a letter to Grandma, have a conversation with our friends, or impress a stranger with our integrity? Once we have learned how to think, we have a responsibility to share what we know. Like the Noble Eightfold Paths of the Buddha, we owe it to our society to build a character that God would be proud to say, "With him I am well pleased." It is our obligation to be as much like our Lord and savior as we can become even though as humans we will always be sinners; he forgives us and will be waiting for us.

Communications Makes the World Go Round; Sharing What We Know:
Once we have learned how to think, we have a responsibility to share what we know. Like the followers of the Noble Eightfold Paths of the Buddha, we owe it to our society to have the type of character that will work every day to make our way of life "doing the right thing." To share, we must communicate. Whether it is a report for our employer, a résumé of our ability and work experience, a newscast, a letter to Grandma,

a presentation or a simple conversation, communications reflect our character, intelligence, wisdom, and capabilities or our lack thereof. St. Paul in First Corinthians 14:7 likens proper communications to music, he says, "If inanimate things that produce sound, such as a flute or harp, do not give out the tones distinctly, how will what is being played on the flute or harp be recognized? And if the bugle gives an indistinct sound, who will get ready for battle? Similarly, if you—because of speaking in tongues—do not utter intelligible speech, how will anyone know what is being said?"

"Communications," says St. Paul, "is the key to understanding. Think about what you don't understand and recognize there may be more that one thought." The act of communication requires a series of thought processes to be considered before the spoken word is given. For example, I have experienced talking to people who aren't listening. They are thinking about, instead, what they are going to say next without consideration to what I have just said to them. They are the type of people who know the answer before hearing the question. A one-way conversation is not very meaningful to anyone. One should be a listener before becoming a talker.

What gives communications its significance is the value of the message and how effectively it is presented. Therefore, the first characteristic of effective communications is the way the words in the message are put together; this is known as its grammatical style. The type of grammatical style we use may very well determine what social and intellectual class of society one belongs. Therefore, care should be taken to understand one's audience before any attempts to communicate are undertaken. Part of our social credentials consists of how well we speak our language, because of this, one's grammatical style is very much a part of our social makeup. Whether you subscribe to the vernacular used by Mark Twain's *Huckleberry Finn* or the grammatical efficiency of old English, there are those who have the talent to adjust their style according to their audience. The audience you are speaking or writing to must understand what you say or write. Even though you may not subscribe to the simplistic style of Steinbeck's Joe Valery, "Don't believe nobody, the bastards are after you," and "Put your faith in dough. Everybody wants it, everybody will sell out for it." We get the message, but unless you want the reputation of Joe's character, you should learn to communicate with a little more accuracy and class.

We first learn about grammar in grade school and continue to learn its rules and usage through high school. One of the first things we learned is what makes a sentence. First, the sentence must be talking about something called a subject. Next, the subject has to be doing something, which is called the predicate or the verb in action, and finally, the sentence must make sense. If these three things are present, the sentence is said to contain a complete thought and be an independent clause.

On the other hand, if the sentence is correct, the word might be wrong. For example, you want to explain the effects of an event, but first, you have to state the cause. The effect (not affect) is produced by the consequence of an action. The principal cause of the effect the speech had was due to the effect the principal made on the students when he explained the rules. For example: The new rules will not affect me. Notice the use of the four words *affect, effect principle*, and *principal. Effect* means caused; *affect* is the influence the effect had by the principal, who is the head authority of the principles or rules which are to be followed. There are so many rules of grammar and word usage that one must memorize that you can go nuts. *On* indicates the time of an occurrence, for example, and *of* should not be used in place of *have. Between* refers to two, and *among* deals with three or more. Then there is the word *cites*, or is it *sight*, or is it *site*? Let's see, *sight* refers to see, *site* deals with a location, and *cite* is to quote someone or is to accuse someone of a legal infraction. If you need to know whether to use *who* or *whom*, you have to ask, who did it or for whom it was done? Substitute *he = who* and *him = whom*.

Communications, whether it is written or oral, requires interpretations to be made, which reduces what we understand to knowledge and a set of rules; therefore, there is sometimes a learning gap between the communicator and the interpreter caused by differences in education, experience, vocabulary, interest, morals, and character. When you really think about it, art, music, literature, law, and philosophy all need to be interpreted to get the most benefit from its message. The degree to which it is understood by one to another is dependent on whether or not it has been communicated in a manner that can be understood based on the education of the receiver. Sentences are supposed to express thoughts, have a relationship of ideas in a declaration, a question, a command, a wish, a prayer, or an exclamation. The shorter or less information you make either end of the communication or interpretation, the less likely it will produce, for the receiver, an authoritative conclusion.

When I ask high school students a question, which requires a written answer, I usually get the shortest answer possible. For example, I might ask, "What point of view did the author use to write his story?" Their first choice is first person, which may be the correct answer, but it lacks depth—both of us have to understand who and what we are talking about, besides, I can't tell if they read the story or saw it on the dustcover. Their second choice for an answer is autobiographical—same thing, the answer is correct, but because it lacks depth, I cannot tell if they read it or not. The better choice would be something like this:

> Mr. Lionel Garcia uses the first person point of view in his autobiographical story about his many humorous and interesting childhood experiences playing baseball.

Now I know the author's name: Lionel Garcia
Point of view: first person
Genre: autobiographical
Something about the subject: childhood experiences playing baseball.

The student probably read the story, but more questions need to be answered to know for sure. After reading the next story, I might ask, "How does the author's writing style in *Baseball* differ from the style used in *One Writer's Beginning*?"

Students write:

> One is about how baseball was played when the writer was growing up and the other is about the author's learning how to write a better story.

The question concerned the author's style of writing not the subject matter. I think the students took for granted that the reader would assume that both stories were written by the author as autobiographical accounts of their youth. The preferable answer would be:

> Both stories are autobiographical accounts of childhood experiences. In *Baseball*, Mr. Garcia writes more like a narrator telling us how he and his friends played the game while Eudora Wetty in *One Writer's Beginnings* uses the first person pronouns, *I*, *we*, and *my* to clearly indicate that the piece is an autobiographical and to interject her own thoughts and opinions about the subject matter.

Another possibility would be:

> Even though both stories are autobiographical accounts of each author's childhood experiences, Mr. Garcia's *Baseball* is more descriptive, while *One Writer's Beginnings*, by Eudora Wetty, is written as a personal experience that reveals her sensory perceptions and imagination, which lead her to learn a valuable lesson about becoming a better writer. "Always be sure you get your moon in the right part of the sky," her critic told her.

The point I want to make in these examples is, read the question! What does the question want you to answer? You should always be careful to address the question with a specific use of examples, stay away from abstract words and phrases, and be satisfied that you have answered the question. In the examples above, the questions asked were for specific information and should have been addressed factually. I think the students assumed that they had answered the question because they alluded to the fact that both stories were autobiographical when they wrote, "How baseball was played when the writer was growing up" and "the author's learning how to write a better story." The key words they wanted you to pick up on included "when the writer was growing up" and "the author's learning how to write a better story." Although it is true, the author himself or herself knows their experiences better than anyone else, the problem with their assumptive logic—on the part of the reader—of their answers is that anyone could have been telling the story about the authors when they were growing up. In this case, you would have to read the stories yourself to know that they were clearly written in the first person point of view, and therefore, since they were personal experiences, they were autobiographical in genre. I think conversations and writing talents can be improved by learning the elements of writing—what they are, how they are used, and the effectiveness of their use. Again, like grammar, these are taught beginning in sixth grade and are dealt with through high school and on into college if your major is English. Another important aspect of writing or speaking is to deal with the question and present your points clearly. Knowing what is expected of you will help you prepare your response.

Writing Styles:
The types of writing styles that you should be familiar with include:
- *Narrative*: this tells a story about a personal experience.
- *Expository*: it explains ideas or information in detail.
- *Research*: it explores all evidence dealing with a particular subject that leads to a specific conclusion.
- *Persuasive*: used by politicians; supports an opinion or position.
- *Biographical*: tells the story of a real person's life.
- *Assessment*: it gives a clear and complete account of how something works or why something happened.

Remember, opinions are not wrong. I tell my kids, you have the right to say what you think about anything, but what you say regarding your opinion is only acceptable if you make a well-documented presentation of your ideas. However, even in the best presentation, your opinion may not be acceptable to everyone but should be respected by most if it is supported and presented properly.

Writing Techniques:
You should also learn how to use the following techniques in your conversations and writing: *compare/contrast*. Here you should present a clear and complete account of how two or more things are alike or different. When you take an issue on an issue, you should present your strongest thoughts to support your position, provide strong examples of concrete facts not abstract points that are too easy to argue about, and summarize your main points in the most logical way beginning with a statement and building to a strong conclusion. Researching and knowing the facts makes communicating less argumentative, leaving less room

for interpretive guessing about your position and strengthens your evaluation of the subject. Taking a position on an issue and presenting your strongest reasons to support your opinion requires organization. You should begin with a clear and complete account of how you arrived at the conclusions you are presenting. To demonstrate an effective point of view on the issue requires the best use of appropriate examples, reasons, and other evidence to support your position.

Nonfiction
Some of the more common characteristics of nonfiction writing include comparing and contrasting, for example, you may come across a question on a test that asks: Compare and contrast the cultural trends of the 1950s with those of the 1990s. A time line is often included in the presentation as well as an explanation of the cause and effect. Events during one time period often influence the events occurring later, therefore, explaining the cause and effect of one period or exploring the problems societies have faced and the solutions they have sought are a common way to make a presentation of different time periods or events. Nonfiction requires your presentation to be well organized and clearly focused on the subject by demonstrating an accurate, clear, and smooth progression of ideas or the events as they influenced the results.

You could be asked, by your employer, to write an analytical paper regarding the possible effects that the implementation of a new procedure being considered would have on the company's workforce. The first requirement for this kind of analytical paper would be to gather information from all sources available—written, oral, and visual—that will produce the necessary information to support several different possibilities, good and bad. If your boss is in favor of the new idea, you may find yourself caught between the devil and the deep blue sea, especially if your personal conclusions are negative. However, the best policy is to be fair and honest in your presentation. You need to keep in mind that the purpose of the report is to present a logical argument, which offers an opinion on the question, "What effect would the policy being considered have on the successful achievement of company goals?" In this presentation, you are dealing with a cause and effect type of presentation. Research regarding the success or failure of such a policy in other similar companies would be very helpful. Again, the presentation should be concrete and not abstract so thatOhe opportunity for unnecessary debate is avoided. Pros and cons should be part of the presentation so that the audience will not be thinking of why this policy will not work instead of staying focused on the positive features, which would be beneficial to the company. You should make an outline for your presentation before practicing its delivery. A possible outline could be:

1. Introduction: consists of the points you wish to make.
   a. Explains the topic
   b. Presents the points you want to make
   c. Includes a specific statement that states your position
   d. A statement of conclusion that you will demonstrate.

2. Thesis: restates the topic and states the point of the presentation

3. Body: this is the heart of your presentation:
   a. Each main point is discussed, explained, and argued and is used to describe your conclusions, what experiences the same type of policy, within similar companies, has been implemented and the results achieved.
   b. There needs to be a smooth transition from one point to the next.

4. Conclusion:
   a. Sums up your conclusions by providing final thoughts on the subject.

During my pastoral ministry studies, my professor asked the class to consider what the basic elements of our worldview are. I think it represents the type of questions one on the college level could be expected to answer; it is presented here as an example:

While it is true that our understanding of history dramatically affects the way we understand our obligations for shaping the course of social events, it is also true—in terms of understanding the general themes of Catholic social teachings (i.e., God's justice, the dignity of persons, the common good, and the preferential option for the poor)—that we usually carry about with us a basic sense of security or anxiety about ourselves and about life in general, which influences our worldview.

These expectations usually have their roots in specific life experiences, often from childhood. Generally, these experiences end up shaping our expectation about the whole of life, the universe, what it will become, and our relationship to it, and our expectations mature pursuant to our education. By the way, we are influenced by our peers, teachers, friends, and parents and come to light as we continually experience life in our social setting.

In light of these comments, what are the basic elements of your worldview?

A strong Christian faith, supported by the belief that evil does not have the last word, influences the basic elements of my worldview. I believe my Christian faith calls for me to have and maintain a respect for the dignity of persons based on an understanding of God's redemptive grace. It is also my belief that God's justice is revealed most fully in the death and resurrection of Christ and that all of God's promises are valid because of the Divine Revelation. When I examine the world's religions and major philosophies, I see a respect for life and justice surrounded by love at the core of all thought and the principles, which teach doing the right thing conquers all other methods for finding answers to unanswerable questions.

Communication in the Age of Electronics Is Just Beginning:
More states are considering passing legislation that will prohibit texting and using cell phones while driving. Why do we need to legislate our communications? Is this another thing we need a law to go into effect in order to stop an abusive behavior from killing people? How many deaths will it take before the guilty parties get the picture? I wonder if they will come up with a voice text apparatus, which requires no hands, like you have with cell phones in cars. However, how do you dial the number? Maybe the computer does that too. In one of the classrooms at the high school, a teacher has printed on the back wall, "Everyday, somebody, somewhere, does something great . . . Is today your day?" It seems to me that we need one below it that says, "Don't Do Something Stupid Today, Otherwise They'll Pass a Law That Says It's Illegal to Do So."

The twentieth century will no doubt be known in history as the "communication age." News commentators are saying, "Access to information, is access to power." We cannot watch a car go down the road without somebody talking or texting on a cell phone. E-mails are changing the volume of letters going through the post offices, which has caused the price of stamps to go up in price. Nerds are becoming millionaires, and the media can influence the outcome of elections. Computers have given the common person access to information, which was formerly not available to everyone. Global communications is "the process by which national economies, politics, cultures, and societies become integrated with those of other nations around the world has made more products and services available to greater numbers of people." **(8)** Knowing how to use proper grammar is giving way to knowing how to navigate around the Web and completing the requested information to download data.

Therefore, we come to the end of one era and give way to the beginnings of another; that's the way life is. I was rather taken back the other day when I learned that there were some high school students who didn't know what a typewriter was. I only hope we will keep God in our life and continue to "just do what's right!"

I think the moral of the story is "learn all you can." In today's global society, the more you have to offer, the more valuable you will become. In the future, government will no longer be able to support people with few skills, no retirement, less education, empty cupboards, and no health insurance. In a few years, there will be three retired workers for everyone who has a job. Because of the financial crisis Wall Street caused, the scams of crooks whose greed literally caused many to lose all their savings and retirement benefits. With the two wars, a ten percent unemployment rate, and the ridiculous amounts of money our government spends trying to pay for better times to reappear, we will have a hard time being able to recoup our image as the world's mentor. As the world turns today, there are thousands who hate us and see us as people who think they are below our dignity. The irony is when the chips are down who are the first ones to come knocking with help? That's doing the right thing.

THINGS WE SHOULD ALL THINK ABOUT

By supporting public and Christian educational programs, you are helping to build a student who may one day very well become a leader of political importance in our country. Stars are born with talent from God; but good leaders are developed by education, experience, and blessings from God. To be all you can become is to honor your family, your country, yourself, and the God that created you.

In First Corinthians, St. Paul uses the image of the body with its many parts to parallel Christ's relationship with church members, which is made up of many different (parts), i.e., kinds of people. He says, "If one part suffers, all the parts suffer with it; if one part is honored, all parts share its joy." The point becomes, there is diversity in function like each body part has, but no one part is more important than the other without threat to its unity. If the individual members of Christ's church (or body) have its own purpose and function but is fulfilling a unified purpose, we are acting as one body. Love is what holds the spirit (gifts from God) within us for life's distribution. Even when some lose faith because of what they have seen and hope yields to possessions, love never fails according to St. Paul and is the greatest of the three: faith, hope, and love.

The major message of the New Testament seems to be telling us that it is God's love, which is the most important spiritual gift he has given us. When we attempt to live our faith while making everyday choices, love should be at the heart of what it means to be a Christian following in the footsteps of Christ. St. Paul emphasizes that it is love, which unifies church members' lives by understanding; even though there are differences in spirit, they are kept united through communication.

It has been said many times that politics and religion do not mix. Are politicians not Christians? What are the character, morality, and integrity of those who claim not to be Christians but claim to be politicians? There are a lot of communications needed between the two. The Christians need to decide whether the decisions made by politicians are treating our unified purpose. Subjects of interest include judges, who rule on issues such as teaching "intelligent design" whether or not the Ten Commandments can be displayed down at the courthouse, whether or not there is such a thing as abortion rights, and will the Roe v. Wade decision be overturned? What about God and schools, why can't there be electives that deal with world religions? Why is it not allowed to teach intelligent design alongside evolution? What about our foreign human rights issues, famine and aids in Africa, civil war in the Sudan, sex trafficking? Gay marriages, stem cell research, and public displays of religion? Are these issues that need some communications? Can we say Merry Christmas? We need to become better citizens by paying attention to those who represent our interest and ask, is it for the common good? We should become involved in making sure that our Christian values are being represented in political issues and that our representatives have the character, morality, and integrity to sit in the same house that our forefathers built. In a multicultural world, I suppose politics and religion do not mix; but God, like principles, should prevail in our everyday life!

Keep a smile on your face and love in your heart. Peace be with you!

This chapter's ***THINGS WE SHOULD ALL THINK ABOUT*** concentrates on an explanation of the Buddha's Noble Eightfold Path. Most of these follow closely what you would expect from a person with a strong character.

Being Buddhist means there are no threats of hell or promises of heaven. The term *Buddhist* is a class of person and has no inherent existence. The condition of future lives is determined by actions of body speech and mind and not by religious affiliation. **(7)**

The following is truly a man of character.

Have the Right View—This means to try and see things as they really are and not as you want them to be.

Have the Right Intentions—Be always committed to doing what is right.

Use the Right Speech—Do not lie, do not gossip, do not speak with a hateful tone.
Remember, words can hurt people, start wars, and make friends.

Take the Right Action—Do not perform unwholesome acts, act kindly, and be compassionate.
Be honest, respect others and their possessions, and keep sexual relationships harmless to others.

Work with Pride—Do not work in a profession that will hurt others.
For example, avoid dealing in weapons, prostitution, slavery, selling drugs or alcohol, raising animals for slaughter.

Maintain the Right Effort—Effort means nothing can be achieved without the proper effort.
Efforts can be used in either wholesome or unwholesome states. The same type of energy that fuels desire, envy, aggression, and violence can on the other side fuel self-discipline, honesty, benevolence, and kindness.

Right Mindfulness—This is the mental ability to see things as they are with clear consciousness.

Buddha accounted for these as the four foundations of mindfulness:
1. Contemplation of the body
2. Contemplation of feeling (repulsive, attractive, or neutral)
3. Contemplation of the state of mind
4. Contemplation of the phenomena

Right Concentration: This refers to the development of a mental force that occurs in natural consciousness. This refers to wholesome thoughts and actions. By the practice of meditation and right concentration, it becomes natural to apply this method in dealing with everyday situations.

The Five Ethical Precepts and Philosophical Tenets of Zen Buddhism:
- I will not be violent nor will I kill.
- I will respect the property of others; I will not steal.
- I will not give way to lust.
- I will honor honesty and truth; I will not deceive.
- I will exercise proper care of my body and mind. **(8)**

REFERENCES

Introduction:

(1) *The Prophets, An Introduction,* Abraham J. Heschel, Harper Torch books, Harper and Row, Publishers, New York
Anyone wishing to understand the prophet needs to read this book. Heschel writes, "The prophet is a person, not a microphone . . . The prophet's task is to convey a divine view, yet as a person he is a point of view. He speaks from the perspective of God as perceived from the perspective of his own situation . . . The prophet was an individual who said NO to his society, condemning its habits and assumptions, its complacency, waywardness, and syncretism. He was often compelled to proclaim the very opposite of what his heart expected." We should too!

(2) *American Gospel, God, The Founding Fathers and the Making of a Nation*, Jon Meacham, Random House Trade Paperbacks, Random House, Inc. New York 206. p168
This book is necessary reading for anyone interested in the making of a nation. "Think back on the days of old; reflect on the years of age upon age. Ask your father and he will inform you, ask your elders and they will tell you." (Song of Moses, New American Bible Deuteronomy 32:7)

(3) *Memory and Identity, Conversations at the Dawn of a Millennium*, Pope John Paul II, 2005, Rizzoli International Publications, Inc., New York. P.42

Chapter 1: Is It Time To Change

(1) Ariel Cohen Ph.D. is a Senior Research Fellow in Russian and Eurasian Studies and International Energy Security at the Heritage Foundation. He is a member of the Board of Advisers of the Institute for Contemporary Affairs at the Jerusalem Center for Public Affairs. His article, *The Russian-Georgian War: A Challenge for the U.S. and the World*: Can be found at *WWW.heritage.org/Research/Russiaand eurasia/wm2017.cfm*. It was produced by the Douglas and Sarah Allison Center for Foreign Policy Studies. published by the Heritage Foundation 214 Massachusetts Ave NE Washington D.C. 20002-4999.

(2) References used in the presentation include Taubman, William; Sergei Khrushchev and Abbott Gleason (2000) Nikita Khrushchev. Pp16. Pearson, Raymond (2002) The rise and Fall of the Soviet Empire, pp55 Other references are listed on the web cite identified above.

(3) Notes from President Ronald Reagan's speech, "Tear Down This Wall", Brandenburg Gate West Berlin Germany June 12, 1987

(4) Notes from em.wikipedia.org/wiki/Nikita Khrushchev

(5) Dr. Mark J. Perry, Professor of Economics and Finance at the University of Michigan. Study on U.A.W. pay/benefits—Search compensation packages of Detroit Auto Makers and select CARPE DIEW: UAW contracts Put Detroit on Road to Ruin / 11-10-08.

(6) Oklahoma City Catholic Charity letter to interested members explaining the forming of a congregational-based community organization. The model for the organization is based on the Industrial Area Foundation, which is the nation's oldest CBCO network.

(7) CNN Politics.Com. Elections Center 2008 LGBT Issues

(8) Web.MD.Com, American Academy of Child and Adolescent Psychiatry web cite, Facts for Families May 2008.

(9) Daily Oklahoman Newspaper, Sunday, October 5, 2008 Opinion-Our Views/School Truancy.

(10) Chicagotribune.com—Students Add Sabotage to College-Entry Arsenal by Jodi S. Cohen Oct.20, 2008

Chapter Two: The Importance Of Ethics Integrity And Morality In Building A Code Of Conduct

(1) Analects XV: 23,

(2) Analects Chapter X, 1

(3) Analects XV: 23 The Analects are a collection of Confucius' conversations and pronouncements on the proper conduct of Life, which according to tradition were recorded by his disciples soon after is death. The Analects consists of 497 verses and are the closest thing we will ever have to a true picture of the man and his teachings according to Thomas and Dorothy Hoobler in "Confucianism" World Religions, 1993, Facts on File, Inc. 460 Park Ave So. New York City, New York.

(4) Russell, Bertrand, *Philosophical Essays*, London, Routledge, 1994.

(5) Ibid.

(6) Crane, Stephen The Red Badge of Courage and Other Stories, New York, CRW Publishers Limited, 2004,

(7) Ibid.,

(8) Ibid.

(9) All Bible Passages referred to in this chapter are from the *New American Bible, Personal Study Edition* New York. Oxford University Press, 1995

(10) Ellsberg, Robert, editor, *Dorothy Day: Selected Writings* New York, Orbis Books, 1993

(11) Ibid.

(12) Schlessinger, Dr. Laura & Vogel, Rabbi Stewart, *The Ten Commandments, The Significance of God's Laws in Everyday Life,* New York, Harper Publishers, 1998

(13) Banner, William H., *Ethics An Introduction To Moral Philosophy,* New York, Scribner's Sons 1968

(14) Sartre, Jean Paul, *Existentialism*, translated by B. Frechtman, New York Citadal, 1947

(15) Bernstein, Richard J. Ph.D. *John Dewey The Great American Thinkers Series*, New York, Washington Press Edition April 1967

(16) Ibid. (Quote is from "Art as Experience, by John Dewey Capricorn Books, 1934) pp.157-58 *John Dewey*, by Richard J. Bernstein, Ph.D. New York Washington Press 1967.

(17) Melchin, Kenneth R., Living With Other People An Introduction to Christian Ethics Based on Bernard Lonergan. Minnesota, Liturgical Press 1998.

(18) Pope Paul the VI, *Gaudium et Spes, The Church in the Modern World*, Encyclical, Second Vatican Council December 7, 1965 * All Encyclicals may be read at http:www. Newadvent.ord/ index.html

(19) Haig Mich, Marvin L. *Catholic Social Teaching and Movements*, Ct., Twenty Third Publications 2001.

(20) Pacem in Terris, Encyclical on establishing universal peace in Truth, Justice, Charity, and Liberty, His Holiness Pope John xxiii, promulgated on April 11, 1963 (* May be read at http:www. Newadvent.ord/index.html)

(21) Steinbeck, John, *East of Eden*, New York, Penguin Group, Centennial Edition, 2002

(22) Ibid. Living With Other People, Kenneth R. Melchin, An Introduction to Christian ethics based on Bernard Lonergan, Saint Paul University Series in Ethics, The Liturgical Press Collegeville, Mn.

(23) Schlessinger, Dr. Laura and Rabbi Stewart Vogel, *The Ten Commandments, The Significance of God's Law in Everyday Life*, Harper Collins Publishers, New York 1998.

Chapter 3: *Everything Has A Beginning*

(1)   Russell, Bertrand, *What I Believe,* Great Britain, Kegan Paul, Trench, Trubner, 1925

(2)   Tolstoy, Leo, *Confessions*, translated by Louise and Aylmer Maude, Dover Publishing, Jan. 2005

(3)   Fisher, Mark Dr. *The Foundations of Karl Rahner: A Paraphrase of the Foundations of Christian Faith.* The Crossroad Publishing Co., 10-01-05 Note: (Dr. Mark Fisher's synopsis is a must for understanding, The Foundations of Karl Rahner who is considered to be one of Catholicism's most influential theologians.)

(4)   Ibid.

(5)   Goyette, John., Latkovic, Mark S., and Myers, Richard, Editors, *Thomas Aquinas And The Natural Law Tradition,* The Catholic University of America Press, 2004.

(6)   Gert, Bernard, *The Definition of Morality*, The Stanford Encyclopedia of Philosophy (Summer 2005) last modified 8-29-2008.

(7)   Walsh, Thomas, *Religious Freedom and the Moral Society*, a speech delivered at the International Coalition for Religious Freedom Conference on "Religious Freedom and the New Millennium" Washington,D.C. April 17-19, 1998

(8)   Confucius, *The Analects*, translated by D.C. Lau, London, Penguin Books Ltd., 1979.

(9)   Melchin, Kenneth R., *Living With Other People,* Minnesota, The Liturgical Press, 1998.

(10) Ibid.

(11) Gert, Bernard, *The Definition of Morality*, the Stanford Encyclopedia of Philosophy. 2005

(12) Meacham, Jon, *American Gospel*, New York, Alfred A. Knopf. 2007.

(13) Karabell, Zachary, *Peace Be Upon You*, New York, Random House, 2007

(14) Ibid

(15) Ibid

(16) Steinbeck, John, *East of Eden*, Centennial Edition, New York Penguin Books, 2002

(17) Melchin, Kenneth, *Living With Other People,* Minnesota, The Liturgical Press, 1998.

(18) Van Diema, David and Chu, Jeff, *Does God Want You To Be Rich. ?* Time Inc. Sept 11, 2006 Volume 168 No 12, New York.

(19) Schlessinger, Laura Dr. and Vogel, Rabbi Stewart. *The Ten Commandments, The Significance of God's Laws in Everyday Life.* New York Harper Collins, 2005

(20) Bertrand Russell on History, from his Collection of Philosophical Essays, New York, Simon & Schuster, 1967.

Chapter Four: Where and What is God?

(1) Neusch, Marcel, *The Sources of Modern Atheism*, New York, Paulist Press, 1982

(2) Morman, Rev. Kenneth G., Diocese of Toledo, Ohio from *MOTGScript@aol.com.* a study course written for internet study by Rev Morman. He wrote a number of articles during 2002 for this study course.

(3) Schlessinger, Laura and Vogel, Stewart, *The Ten Commandments, the Significance of God's Laws in Everyday Life*. New York, Harper Collins, 1998

(4) Father Kenneth G. Morman, Diocese of Toledo, Ohio from *MOTGScript@aol.com*

(5) Ibid

(6) Ralph, Margaret Nutting, *And God Said What?: an introduction to biblical literary forms,* revised edition New Jersey, Paulist Press, 2003

(7) Ibid

(8) Schlessinger, Laura and Vogel, Stewart, *The Ten Commandments, the Significance of God's Laws in Everyday Life,* New York, Harper Collins, 199 8.

Chapter Five: A Case For Religious Education: Why Do I Need To Belong To A House Of Worship?

(1) Sheard, Robert B., "An Introduction to Christian Belief, A Contemporary Look at the Basics of Faith", Mystic, Ct., Twenty Third Publications, 1996

(2) Rausch, Thomas P. S.J., "The College Student's Introduction to Theology", Minnesota, The Liturgical Press, 1993

(3) Brevilly, Elizabeth; O'Brian, Joanne; Palmer, Martin; "Religion of the World; The Illustrated Guide to Origins, Beliefs, Traditions, and Festivals," Consultant Editor, Professor Martin E. Marty, Facts on File Inc. New York, 1997, Print

(4) Pope Paul VI, "Dogmatic Constitution on Divine Revelation" (Dei Verbum,) November 18, 1965, Rome, The Vatican

(5) Einstein, Albert, The World As I See It, an essay included in Living Philosophies, New York

(6) Simon Schuster, 1931

(7) Barrett, et al, David B., "World Christian Encyclopedia: A Comparative Survey of Churches and Religions in the Modern World," Oxford University Press, 2001.

(8) Durant, Will, "The Age of Faith", New York, Simon & Schuster, 1950

(9) Shelley, Bruce L. "Church History in Plain Language" Nashville, Thomas Nelson, 1995

(10) Keating, Joseph, "Christianity", The Catholic Encyclopedia Vol. 3. New York Robert leton Company., 1908. 25 Nov. 2009. http://newadvent.org./cathen/03712a.htm>.

(11) Lonergan, Bernard, "Method in Theology," 1973 Edition, San Francisco, Harper and Harper, 1984

(12) Russell, Bertrand, "Philosophical Essays", London, Routledge, 1994

(13) Bainton, Roland H., "The Reformation of the Sixteenth Century," Beacon Press, Boston, 1985

(14) Ibid.

(15) Robinson, B.A., "About the Origin of Species and of Life Itself, Creation Science", Ontario Consultants on Religious Tolerance @ Religious Tolerance.org. Web.Cite

(16) Smith, Tom, W., "Classifying Protestant Denominations" quotes from Reverend J. Gordon Melton and Edwin S. Gaustad. Original source. *http://www.icpsr.umich.edu/GSS99/report/m-report/meth43.htm*

(17) Ibid.

(18) Steinbeck, John, "Grapes of Wrath", Viking Press, New York, 1939

(19) Father Kenneth G. Morman, Diocese of Toledo, Ohio from *MOTGScript@aol.com*

(20) Schlessinger, Dr. Laura & Vogel, Rabbi Stewart, *The Ten Commandments, The Significance of God's Laws in Everyday Life,* New York, Harper Publishers, 1998

(21) Father Kenneth G. Morman, Diocese of Toledo, Ohio from *MOTGScript@aol.com*

(22) Holmes, David, "The Faith's of the Founding Fathers." Oxford University Press, New York, 2006

(23) Meacham, Jon, *American Gospel*, New York, Alfred A. Knopf. 2007.

(24) Ibid.

(25) Holmes, David, "The Faith's of the Founding Fathers." Oxford University Press, New York, 2006

(26) Meacham, Jon, *American Gospel*, New York, Alfred A. Knopf. 2007.

(27) Ibid

(28) Ibid.

(29) Holmes, David, "The Faith's of the Founding Fathers." Oxford University Press, New York, 2006

(30) Ibid.

(31) Ibid

(32) Ibid

(33) Simon, Richard Rev., "A Critical History of the Old Testament", Chez Frederic Arnaud, Frankfort, 1684 (First edition of one of the earliest works on the Eastern churches and more important, also one giving a correct description of the tenets of those churches. The second, third and fourth French editions appeared in 1687, 1693 and 1711. An English translation was also published in 1685.
Richard Simon (1638-1712) was a famous Hebraist whose most important work was his critical history of the Old Testament, which caused a lot of criticism and was banned in France. As a consequence all his later works appeared outside of France. Concerning the place of printing of this work, there is some uncertainty about whether it is Frankfurt or Amsterdam, as the British Library states.

(34) Steinbeck, John, *East of Eden*, Centennial Edition, New York, Penguin Books, 2002

(35) Ibid.

(36) Ibid

(37) Durant, Will & Ariel, "The Age of Voltaire", Simon & Schuster, New York, 1965

(38) Rhys, David W., "Dialogue of the Buddha," London, Oxford Press, 1899.

(39) Information concerning the The Noble Eight Fold Path found on the web. site at http//www. hebigview.com/Buddhism/ eightfoldpath.html—The Five Principal Relationships at www.globaled.org/   /chinaproject/confucuan/quotes1.html and the Four Noble Truths at fundamentalbuddhism.com/ four-noble-truths.html

(40) Cather, Willa, "Death Comes for the Arch Bishop", Vintage Classics New York, 1990

(41) "Fr. Athanasius Iskander" *athanas@sympatico.ca* St. Mary's Coptic Orthodox Church, Kitchener, Canada

(42) Brevilly, Elizabeth; O'Brian, Joanne; Palmer, Martin; "Religions of the World; The Illustrated Guide to Origins, Beliefs, Traditions, and Festivals," Consultant Editor, Professor Martin E. Marty, Facts on File Inc. New York, 1997, Print

(43) Crane, Stephen, "The Red Badge Of Courage and Other Stories", New York, CRW Publishers Limited, 2004

(44) Sheard, Robert B., "An Introduction to Christian Belief, A Contemporary Look at the Basics of Faith", Mystic, Ct. Twenty Third Publications, 1996

Chapter 6: Learn All You Can

(1) Shelley, Bruce, "Church History in Plain Language", Third Edition, Nashville, Thomas Nelson, 2008

(2) Steps to Genius Every Day (1998) Delacorte Press) explains how individuals and organizations can apply da Vinci's seven principles to improve Performance Learning Center, Edgewater, New Jersey, in his book: "Seven communication, encourage creative and innovative thinking, and foster a team environment in the work place. Gelb, Michael J. "How To Think Like Leonardo da Vinci," is a must read on the subject of the Seven Steps to Genius Every Day, New York Random House, 2009

(3) The Daily Oklahoman Newspaper Article appearing in the May 24th, 2007 issue from Staff Reports Survey performed by Wilson Research Strategies for Accord Human Resource Company according to the Article

(4) Davis, Kenneth C., "Don't know Much About History", New York, Avon Books, 1999

(5) Lonergan, Bernard, "Topics in Education, Vol. 10 of the Collected Works of Bernard Lonergan, edited by R.M. Doran and F.E. Crown Toronto, University of Toronto Press, 1993

(6) Wolfe, Don M., "Creative Ways to Teach English", New York, The Odyssey Press, Inc. 1959

(7) Information on the Noble Eightfold Path can be found at *http:// www.thebigview.com/buddhism/eightfoldpath.htm*;

(8) Hitchcock, Susan Tyler with Esposito, John L. "Geography of Religion, Where God Lives, Where Pilgrims Walk", National Geographic, Washington, D.C. 2004 is a wonderful reference book on Hinduism, Buddhism, Judaism, Christianity, and Islam with wonderful on site pictures to complement the presentation of the material. The Introduction is penned by Archbishop Desmond Tutu and the Rev. Mpho A. Tutu

INDEX

CPSIA information can be obtained at www.ICGtesting.com
Printed in the USA
LVOW040059061112

305963LV00002B/66/P